To:

_____

From:

_____

Date

_____

Love the life you have

100 WAYS TO EMBRACE GOD'S GOODNESS

JEAN FISCHER

illustrated by NATHALIE OUEDERNI

THOMAS NELSON
Since 1798

Published in Nashville, Tennessee, by Thomas Nelson. Thomas Nelson is a registered trademark of HarperCollins Christian Publishing, Inc.

Thomas Nelson titles may be purchased in bulk for educational, business, fund-raising, or sales promotional use. For information, please email SpecialMarkets@ThomasNelson.com.

ISBN 978-1-4002-1963-6 (hardcover)
ISBN 978-1-4002-1964-3 (ebook)

Printed in China

20 21 22 23 24 GRI 10 9 8 7 6 5 4 3 2 1

Contents

Introduction

I have learned the secret of being
content in any and every situation.

—PHILIPPIANS 4:12

What is true contentment?

The dictionary defines *contentment* as "a feeling of satisfaction with one's possessions, status, or situation." But like the feeling that comes when we pair a cozy novel with a hot beverage on a cold day, that kind of contentment is fleeting. Life interrupts. Life alters contentment, morphing it into discontent, sullenness, or even anxiety.

There's another kind of contentment, a better kind that stays with you all the time. It's called "true contentment," and it cannot be fully described in a dictionary definition. True contentment is trusting the love of our all-powerful, all-good, all-wise God. It is knowing that you aren't traveling life's path alone, that your days aren't meaningless, and that life isn't random. It is believing in the value of the present and having confidence in a joy-filled, eternal future.

Do you believe true contentment is possible? Are you content with your life?

The apostle Paul knew contentment. In Philippians 4:12, he said this: "I have learned the secret of being content in any and every situation." You can learn the secret too. By making a few simple adjustments to your daily life and being intentional about your thought life and your habits, you will learn to live a life of real contentment and peace.

Growing into a state of true contentment is like creating a work of art. It takes skill, imagination, and openness to change. If you are willing, you can create a contentment style all your own, the kind where contentment is possible in *all* circumstances—even during a global crisis. A blank canvas awaits!

Begin by jotting down in a notebook your answers to these questions:

- When do I feel most content? Why am I content there and then?
- In what places of my life—if any—am I at all *not* content, and what prompts or feeds that discontent?
- Am I able to live in the moment? What contributes to that ability or inability?
- Do I have enough, or do I often want more? If the latter, what kinds of things do I tend to want more of?
- Am I able to celebrate the good in my life while working through the bad? Whether you answer yes or no, give an example.

Keep in mind your answers to these questions as you read this book. You'll revisit some common themes throughout these pages. Know that this quest to learn contentment is a lifelong journey. As you create and refine this artistic work of contentment you are cultivating in your life, some of your answers might change. Ideally, the changes will be positive, and you'll be learning along the way.

1

Enjoy the Ride

Life is like a roller coaster. You can either
scream every time there is a bump,
or you can throw your hands up and enjoy the ride.

—UNKNOWN

True contentment is different from a feeling of happiness, joy, or tranquility. In fact, true contentment isn't a feeling at all. It's a state of mind that connects to the deeper, in-your-heart sense that everything is okay, a sense beyond your understanding. Contentment also becomes the lens through which you evaluate your experiences in the world.

Life has its ups and its downs. But when you're living with a God-focused mindset and a heart of contentment, you don't have to be whipsawed as life's crazy events unfold. Instead, you can move forward with faith and peace of mind, knowing that all of these temporary and external events are in the hands of the eternal Sustainer of the universe who numbers the hairs on your head.

True contentment allows you to be okay in the moment—any moment—because you know that whatever happens, whatever challenge life brings your way, by God's grace you will come out okay on the other side.

How often do you bask in the security of knowing that you will always be okay? In our chaotic world, it's not easy to live with an all-the-time secure feeling. But it *is* possible. It just takes practice.

the choice is yours

2

Choose Contentment

Optimism is the faith that leads to achievement.
Nothing can be done without hope.

—HELEN KELLER

You and I are free to choose what we want, what we do, and what we think about. Given that, why do we choose over and over to be anything but content? Seemingly wired into us is the sense that it would be okay to remain in *this* situation, but not be in *that* situation. This book will challenge that thinking.

This requires thinking intentionally and optimistically. I'm reminded of the story of Pollyanna, who went through life playing the Glad Game and teaching everyone around her to do the same. The object of the game was to find the goodness and the beauty that exist in every situation.

Did you get that? *Every* situation. Look to see where in your life you are saying, "Yeah, but there's no goodness or beauty in *this* situation." Are you willing to be honest with yourself about finding some good in that situation anyway? When you begin to go through life knowing deep in your heart—deep in your soul—that there is always something good to find in everything, you begin not to get so worried or stressed when something isn't going your way.

Approaching life intent on looking for the beautiful and maintaining an optimistic attitude can lead to a beyond-understanding, rooted-in-God kind of peace that is infectious and contagious (in the good way). Again, choosing contentment involves practice and faith that the good is out there—and then looking for it. Optimism is something you can cultivate with practice. The choice is yours.

3

Disconnect for a While

---

*The mind is sharper and keener in seclusion and
uninterrupted solitude. Originality thrives in seclusion
free of outside influences beating upon us to cripple
the creative mind. Be alone; that is the secret of
invention: be alone, that is when ideas are born.*

—NIKOLA TESLA

Smartphones allow you to talk and text with your friends. The internet gives you instant access to the ever-expanding world of online media. Today, there's an app for just about everything. If your smartphone has become your constant companion, ask yourself, "Am I more connected with the outside world than I am with my family, with myself, and with God?" If your answer to any part of that question is yes, then you might consider breaking up with media—at least for a while.

According to an article published in 2018 by Nielsen Media Research, the average adult in the United States spends over eleven hours a day interacting with media—and *media* here includes social networking, games, music, reading, streaming TV, and movies. *Eleven hours!* That's nearly half a day! That's almost two-thirds of a person's waking hours! That's TMMI—too much media information!

Such an extreme connection to the world shifts your thoughts away from the things you truly want. So, be careful about how much media and social media you consume. For the next week, use your phone and computer only when necessary—and try to stay off social media altogether. You could even consider turning off the television. Use these fasts to spend more time with your family or get closer to God. Maybe spend time out in nature and in awe of God's miraculous creation all around you. Do something creative. Also, decide how regular, intentional breaks from media might contribute to your becoming more content.

If you want practice in finding the good, here are six things you can choose to do right now to disconnect and turn your attitude around:

1. Get your nose out of the news. Nothing squashes optimism more than a litany of all the bad things happening in the world. Be aware of what's going on, but don't allow the news to ruin your day. Be deliberate about how much media and social media you consume.
2. Spend time with positive people. Learn from them. Ask them about the life experiences that helped shape their positive perspectives.
3. Be aware when you start to complain and instead look for the silver lining.
4. Rather than focus on your problems, brainstorm creative solutions.
5. Remember that most problems are temporary, mere bumps in the road.
6. Believe there is light at the end of the tunnel. Expect something good in the future.

4

Check Your Perspective

If the doors of perception were cleansed, everything
would appear to man as it is, infinite.

—WILLIAM BLAKE

A farmer lived in a tiny house with his wife, a dozen children, and his mother-in-law. The noise in the house bothered the farmer so much that he sought counsel from his rabbi.

"Rabbi, what should I do?" the farmer asked.

"Move your chickens and roosters into the house," the rabbi told him.

The farmer followed the rabbi's advice, but the noise was still too much. Again, he went to the rabbi.

"Move your goats inside," the rabbi suggested.

The farmer did what he was told—and the goats just made things worse. He hurried back to his teacher, seeking more wisdom.

The rabbi told him, "Move in your cow."

The farmer added his cow to the ever-growing menagerie inside the house. Now the noise from the animals crowing, clucking, bleating, and bellowing along with the humans complaining was unbearable! The farmer was stepping on eggs and worrying about goats eating clothes off the clothesline—it was all too much for him.

"Rabbi, what should I do?" he wailed.

"Get the animals out of your house," the rabbi said.

So the farmer went home and did what the rabbi said. And the farmer discovered that the everyday sounds of his wife, all those children, and even his mother-in-law were like music to his ears.

This simple fable offers great insight. Maybe you've added animals to your house without even realizing it. Have you brought home worries and negative thoughts—and allowed them to breed? May the farmer's tale remind you to quiet the noise, because quiet is another precondition of true contentment. Remember when life gets noisy, God is in control—even if it doesn't seem like it.

Hope
is the thing
with
feathers

5
Add a Little Hope

Hope sees the invisible, feels the intangible,
and achieves the impossible.

—HELEN KELLER

Hope is another important contributor to true contentment. Hope is the God-given confident expectation of something good happening. Hope steps out in faith as it looks ahead to the future. If you allow it, hope will lead you to restful contentment even in the darkest times.

Be inspired by looking ahead today! Add a generous amount of hope to your mindset and watch your contentment increase.

"HOPE" IS THE THING WITH FEATHERS

"Hope" is the thing with feathers-
That perches in the soul,
And sings the tune without the words,
And never stops-at all-
And sweetest-in the Gale-is heard;
And sore must be the storm-
That could abash the little Bird
That kept so many warm.
I've heard it in the chillest land,
And on the strangest Sea;
Yet-never-in Extremity,
It asked a crumb-of me.

—*Emily Dickinson (1830–1886)*

KEEP IN
THE SUNLIGHT

6

Banish the What-Ifs

Do not anticipate trouble, or worry about what
may never happen. Keep in the sunlight.

—BENJAMIN FRANKLIN

When you notice a what-if entering your mind, that's not *your* thought. Contentment's archenemy, Fear, and his brother, Worry, are speaking.

What if I get into an accident? What if my child gets sick? What if I end up alone? What if I never find my dream job? What if I lose my job?

What-ifs increase fear, and fear endeavors to sap all your confidence by causing worry. But you were created with everything you need to conquer fear.

Occasionally—although rarely—fear is warranted. If the weather map shows record-breaking hurricane winds approaching, fear of its power will demand your attention and compel you to act. But even then, fear doesn't have to paralyze you or rob you of your deep sense of contentment rooted in the truth that God is in charge.

The fear prompted by what-ifs, however, is fear of the highly unlikely things that will probably never happen. When a what-if situation does occur— the car accident, the appendicitis, or the unannounced company arriving for three days—we are called simply to be responsible; we are to respond. And when you know you're capable of responding to life's less-than-wonderful surprises, you are definitely learning contentment.

Bottom line: fear and contentment cannot live in the same heart. One of them has to go. Try replacing fearful thoughts with hope-filled truth.

7

Take Time to Reflect

Reflect upon your present blessings of which
every man has many—not on your past
misfortunes, of which all men have some.

—CHARLES DICKENS

Imagine yourself sometime in the future feeling content and serenely saying, "Life is so good!"

Today, perhaps the road to true contentment looks long, and your plans are fuzzy. If so, don't let that discourage you. After all, you are a beautiful work in progress. And each day you can make positive changes that will help you move even closer to that serene state of contentment.

When an artist is in the middle of a project, she often takes breaks to reflect on what she's done so far and consider what she wants to do next. Do that now. Take a few minutes to think for a while about where you've found contentment in the past. Take time to answer these questions:

- What are three of the happiest moments in your life?
- Which little indulgences have given you the greatest pleasure?
- What special place brought you a sense of peace?
- When did someone's words warm your heart?
- What items of clothing have made you feel your best?
- What is the best aroma of something cooking ever to come out of your kitchen?

- When, if ever, has the beauty of nature made you stop what you were doing and marvel at what you saw?
- When, if ever, has prayer or some other spiritual practice helped you feel safe and secure? Be specific.
- What accomplishment in life brought you the greatest satisfaction?
- When have you felt blessed? Be specific about one or two times.

Each moment of contentment is a blessing, and every blessing is a brush-stroke. The blessings you experienced in the past can become the backdrop of your picture of true peace. Each stroke, one after the other, adds to your artistic work of contentment.

8

Harvest Your Holy Spirit Fruit

A branch cannot produce fruit alone
but must remain in the vine.
In the same way, you cannot produce
fruit alone but must remain in me.

—JOHN 15:4 NCV

Contentment comes when you have the confidence that you are cultivating certain godly behaviors in your life. Paul listed these qualities in Galatians 5:22–23 (NASB) and called them "the fruit of the Spirit":

- Love
- Joy
- Peace
- Patience
- Kindness
- Goodness
- Faithfulness
- Gentleness
- Self-control

When we—to quote Paul—"walk by the Spirit" (v. 16) and yield to His work in our hearts as well as His guidance in our days, these traits Paul listed will be more obvious in us. Although we can decide, for instance, to be kind or patient, the Holy Spirit enables us to be kinder or more patient than we could be in our own power. We will have a positive impact on people we encounter. We will be more effective in emergency what-ifs, and we will be composed with clear thinking through difficult circumstances. And living out these Holy Spirit traits will greatly contribute to our overall sense of contentment.

9

Fall in Love

You can't blame gravity for falling in love.

—ALBERT EINSTEIN

Imagine a busy city street at rush hour. Cars are stuck in webs of traffic, exhaust fumes poison the air, horns honk, and pedestrians dodge trucks and buses. Life without love would be much like that: a noisy, tangled, life-draining mess of discontent.

And when discontent arises—whether it's because of work, or laundry, or traffic, or any difficult situation—love is the very thing that can defuse discontent, bring sweetness, and help you remember why you're doing the things you're doing, whether for yourself or for the people in your life.

That's why I encourage you to fall in love. Fall in love with everything you have rather than looking at what everyone else has. Fall in love with everything you do. Develop a deep appreciation for the people in your life as well as for your home, your health, and your daily routine.

I heard a woman share about how much she hated putting on her makeup every morning. She hated the cost of the cosmetics, the time it took to do it and get it right, and the fact that she felt like she *had* to put on makeup to fit in. Then one day she got tired of feeling that way, so she changed her way of thinking about it. She decided that this part of each morning would be a sacred time. She would neatly lay out all of her brushes, set out the color palettes available to her, and, instead of feeling like she had to cover up her face, she would treat her face like a new canvas—and she was the artist. She fell in love with this part of her day.

You can do this too. You can change your way of thinking about anything! As you look at your life, where can you fall in love? Where can you create a sacred space? As your love grows, so will your tolerance for all things that would normally upset you. And soon to follow are greater contentment and peace, more creativity and joy.

Love helps you cope with chaos and endure life's noise. Consider each new day a fresh canvas on which to paint, and you're the artist.

10

Live in Love

No man truly has joy unless he lives in love.

—SAINT THOMAS AQUINAS

Your spouse left the toilet seat up . . . *again.* Your kids are shrieking, wailing, and screaming . . . for no good reason. The dog tracked mud onto the kitchen floor . . . that you had just finished cleaning. And now your sister texts that she's on her way over. *Make it stop!*

Left unchecked, little things snowball into bigger messes. And those little things combined with relationship issues can definitely threaten love.

In 1 Corinthians 13:4–7, Paul described love:

Love is patient and kind. Love is not jealous, it does not brag, and it is not proud. Love is not rude, is not selfish, and does not get upset with others. Love does not count up wrongs that have been done. Love takes no pleasure in evil but rejoices over the truth. Love patiently accepts all things. It always trusts, always hopes, and always endures. (NCV)

When you work at living out Paul's definition of love, life's little annoyances don't seem as big. Begin by practicing patience and kindness. Use sticky notes to remind you. Pray. Ask God to help you become more patient and kinder, especially on days when contentment seems far away. When you choose the path of love from 1 Corinthians 13:4–7, you'll not only improve your relationships, but you'll also help make the world a better place—and guess what? *Your* quality of life improves. Everyone wins!

11

Write a Love Letter

Love does not dominate; it cultivates.

—JOHANN WOLFGANG VON GOETHE

Encounters with people can definitely affect how we think about ourselves. But how often are our own thoughts about ourselves also doing some damage?

What if, instead of feeling bad as a result of other people's words or even your own words to yourself, you did something different?

What if you wrote a love letter . . . to yourself? Take a moment to consider:

What do you like about your physical appearance? Is it the color of your hair? The flecks of light in your eyes? The arch of your eyebrows? Your wistful smile?

What aspects of your personality do you like? Is it your compassion? Generosity? Sense of humor? Work ethic?

What special skills do you have? Is it working with children? Coaching sports teams? Throwing together a last-minute meal that is suitable for royalty?

What are some things that you appreciate about yourself that maybe no one even knows about? Perhaps it's the way you meticulously keep your calendar. Or the way you can casually toss flowers into a vase and have them look professionally arranged. Or the way you care for an elderly parent.

Do you see now that you could say a lot in a love letter to yourself? Make it a monthly practice to write yourself a love letter, acknowledging how fearfully and wonderfully God made you and thanking Him for all you are.

Consider this a bit of mental housekeeping—and a step toward being content with how God made you.

—29—

12

Trust God's Timing

Patience is bitter, but its fruit is sweet.

—JEAN-JACQUES ROUSSEAU

What makes you lose your patience? Is it waiting in long lines? Trying to figure out a computer glitch? Friends who always show up late? Little annoyances can become big frustrations. We expect life to run smoothly, and when it doesn't, our tolerance evaporates, and our discontent soars.

Impatience and contentment are like darkness and light: they can't exist simultaneously in the same place. Impatience is saying to others, "My time is more valuable than yours." Impatience is saying to God, "My timing is better than Yours." Impatience makes us act like little children running ahead of our parents even though they tell us to wait. Impatience is self-centered, and it can even be arrogant. It leads us to be inconsiderate of others. Instead of putting them ahead of ourselves, we impatiently regard others as nothing more than obstacles in our way, and this attitude reveals the selfishness of our hearts.

Patience, on the other hand, is a fruit of the Spirit's presence within us that fosters contentment. Patience stops when God says, "Wait." It lets go of selfishness and loves others even when they don't deserve it. Patience tears down attitudes of complaining and disrespect. Above all, patience trusts that God has a reason for you to be right where you are in that long line, or working out the computer glitch, or waiting for your friends.

Now, think of a time when you felt impatient. Why did you struggle to be patient? Name something good that came out of your waiting.

13

Be Kind

The smallest of kindness is worth more
than the greatest intention.

—KAHLIL GIBRAN

Kindness is learned—and it's never too late to learn.

Children who learn to be helpful and considerate, who do little acts of kindness—like opening doors for others, writing thank-you notes, and speaking words of encouragement—become kind, caring adults. And every act of kindness has the potential to prompt another . . . and another . . . and another . . .

Open your eyes. Look all around you. Opportunities to practice kindness are everywhere. And when you recognize someone in need and step in to help, it brings you nearer to others and makes you an essential part of your community—and *that* leads to great contentment.

What is at least one act of kindness you could do today? Make it your goal today to bring more kindness into the world.

14

Do Well by Doing Good

Don't judge each day by the harvest you
reap, but by the seeds that you plant.

—ROBERT LOUIS STEVENSON

Read through these twenty acts of kindness. What are a couple you could do
today—and maybe every day?

1. Tell your loved ones you love them.
2. Return a stray cart from the parking lot.
3. Buy coffee for the person behind you in the drive-through.
4. Leave a thank-you note for a restaurant server.
5. Give a police officer a gift card to a local restaurant.
6. Share your umbrella.
7. Take a new coworker to lunch.
8. Thank a veteran.
9. Spend time with an elderly family member or friend.
10. Offer to carry someone's bags.
11. Buy a meal for a homeless person.
12. On a hot day, give a bottle of cold water to the mail carrier.
13. Send a pizza to your neighborhood fire department.
14. Thank someone who made a difference in your life.
15. Give a small business a glowing recommendation.
16. Write a positive comment on a blog.
17. Drive past a good parking space.

18. Take in your neighbor's garbage can from the curb.
19. Encourage someone who is having a bad day.
20. Make someone laugh.

As you focus this week on being kind, see if your being kind helps you to feel happier and more content.

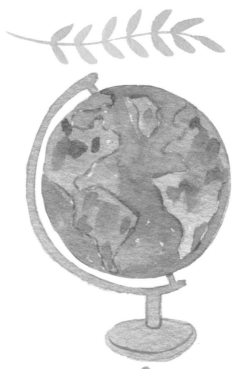

the choices
you make
affect the world

15

Be an Example of Goodness

Virtue is bold, and goodness never fearful.

—WILLIAM SHAKESPEARE

The choices you make affect the world. If you choose to do what others perceive as good or worthy or cool, it can rob you of the treasure of contentment. But when you do what's good and right—even when it's not popular—you'll find contentment.

Also, when you do the right thing—the good thing—you'll never have to look over your shoulder wondering when you might be found out. Doing the good and virtuous thing also affords you a wealth of confidence as that's a win for your well-being, and when you continue doing this day after day, your confidence builds. And when your confidence builds, so does your contentment.

A life lived with virtue and integrity is a life of peace, joy, freedom, and, yes, contentment. Be an example of what it's like to live truly content with your life. Others will take notice and perhaps be inspired by it.

Think today about where you can be an example of goodness. Then go out and make a difference at home, in your community, and even in the world.

Peace
is always
beautiful

16

Embrace the Gift of Peace

I do not want the peace which passeth understanding.
I want the understanding which bringeth peace.

—HELEN KELLER

Where do you find peace? Maybe there is a special place in your home or community where you go for solitude, or perhaps you find peace in a loved one's embrace.

Or is peace more of a "when" for you? Is it a certain time of day? Perhaps it's having morning coffee before everyone else wakes up, or listening to music during an easy commute, or a Saturday with nothing scheduled.

Peace is something we mistakenly search for; to go looking for it often causes frustration. Peace can also feel elusive and fleeting. Like a cool breeze, it refreshes for a moment and then moves on.

But there is a kind of peace that has staying power. This peace is a gift from Jesus, so its roots are divine: "Peace I leave with you; my peace I give you. I do not give to you as the world gives. Do not let your hearts be troubled and do not be afraid" (John 14:27). Jesus walked this earth; He knew how difficult life can be. He therefore offers His followers—then and now—peace rooted in the truth that God is all-powerful, all-loving, and all-wise.

The apostle Paul described Jesus as "our peace" (Ephesians 2:14). He is the reason we can have peace with God: He bridged the infinite gap between holy God and sinful us.

So now, blessed to know peace with God and blessed by the peace Jesus gives His followers, we can be peacekeepers and peacemakers in a world that tends to be a little low on peace.

17

Be at Peace

Peace cannot be kept by force; it can only
be achieved by understanding.

—ALBERT EINSTEIN

Are you familiar with the fable by Aesop about the town mouse and the country mouse? If so, read it again with fresh eyes. As you read the following story, let the simplicity of the message move through you and see what you discover for yourself about contentment in your own situation.

Now you must know that a Town Mouse once upon a time went on a visit to his cousin in the country. He was rough and ready, this cousin, but he loved his town friend and made him heartily welcome. Beans and bacon, cheese and bread, were all he had to offer, but he offered them freely. The Town Mouse rather turned up his long nose at this country fare, and said: "I cannot understand, Cousin, how you can put up with such poor food as this, but of course you cannot expect anything better in the country; come you with me and I will show you how to live. When you have been in town a week you will wonder how you could ever have stood a country life." No sooner said than done: the two mice set off for the town and arrived at the Town Mouse's residence late at night. "You will want some refreshment after our long journey," said the polite Town Mouse, and took his friend into the grand dining-room. There they found the remains of a fine feast, and soon the two mice were eating up jellies and cakes and all that was nice. Suddenly they heard growling and barking. "What is that?" said the Country Mouse. "It is only the dogs of the house," answered the other. "Only!" said the Country Mouse. "I do not like that music at my dinner." Just at that moment the door flew open, in came two huge mastiffs, and the two mice had to scamper down and run off. "Goodbye, Cousin," said the Country Mouse, "What! going so soon?" said the other. "Yes," he replied;

"Better beans and bacon in peace than cakes and ale in fear."

18

Master Self-Control

Self-control is the chief element in self-respect,
and self-respect is the chief element in courage.

—THUCYDIDES

Those doughnuts your coworker brought in to work look delicious. But you promised yourself: no sugar. You've been watching them disappear, and now you're looking at the last one. *Come on. One little doughnut. What's the harm?*

Temptation's voice is cajoling and persistent. That's why self-control requires discipline. Mastering self-control can be difficult, but as you do climb this ladder of discipline, you will find great freedom.

Back to giving up the metaphorical doughnut, this might be uncomfortable in the moment unless we recognize the decision point as a choice between momentary comfort and greater contentment. Giving in to temptation can kill contentment. The key to not giving in—the key to building self-control—lies in knowing your weaknesses.

What area of life would you like to strengthen? When you acknowledge where you are weak, you can begin to build strength in that area. And when you develop self-control in those areas, true contentment follows.

Also, part of developing self-control in those areas where you're feeling weak is forgiving yourself. Today is a new day. Remember that you start every morning with a clean slate.

One more thought. Self-control is trading what you want right now for something better in the future. You are choosing between a temporary craving and what you want *most*. Decide today to make that trade for your future you.

19

Adjust Your Sails

We cannot direct the wind, but we can adjust the sails.

—UNKNOWN

When the wind turns, sailors know how to adjust their sails to stay on course. In life, mastering self-control is learning to adjust your sails when things aren't going as planned or when you face challenging situations. Self-control is a lot like a muscle: the more often you exercise it, the more easily it comes—and with that self-control, contentment comes more readily.

Think about it. When you face a temptation and stop to consider it rather than immediately act, an internal debate begins. *Should I, or shouldn't I?* If you give in, the debate will end, but often guilt and disappointment in yourself follows. And that's not contentment at all.

So make a commitment and have a game plan for what you'll do in a tempting situation. Having these in place will help to eliminate the internal debate. Without a plan, though, you'll find fighting temptation is like fighting the wind.

When self-control wears thin, find a distraction. Read. Exercise. Call a friend. Meditate and pray. Tell yourself "I can" instead of "I can't." Focus on what future goal is important to you right now. Is eating that doughnut more important than eating healthy? Then reward yourself for resisting. (No, not with the doughnut.) When you triumph over temptation, treat yourself to something you enjoy.

20

Practice the Art of Gentleness

Nothing is so strong as true gentleness.
Nothing is so gentle as true strength.

—JOHANN WOLFGANG VON GOETHE

Have you ever seen gentleness de-escalate a tense situation? If so, maybe you were the source of that gentleness.

The Bible tells us that a gentle answer can calm a person's anger (Proverbs 15:1). Gentleness almost always contributes to contentment as well as peace.

Throughout His life, Jesus showed us by His example the power of gentleness. See in Matthew 11:29 the way He described Himself: "Accept my teachings and learn from me, because I am gentle and humble in spirit, and you will find rest for your lives" (NCV). And consider His gentleness with a woman caught in adultery. The Pharisees and teachers of the law were ready to stone her in accordance with Jewish law. Then Jesus made this simple statement: "Let any one of you who is without sin be the first to throw a stone at her" (John 8:7). When no one did, when each one walked away, Jesus was alone with the woman. To her He said simply, "Go and sin no more" (v. 11 NLT).

Choose gentleness today. Refrain from judging others. Treat the people you encounter the way you would like them to treat you, the gentle way your Good Shepherd treats you.

Psalm 23 is perhaps the most beautiful expression of Jesus' gentle ways with us:

The LORD is my shepherd, I lack nothing.
He makes me lie down in green pastures,
he leads me beside quiet waters,
he refreshes my soul.
He guides me along the right paths
for his name's sake.
Even though I walk
through the darkest valley,
I will fear no evil,
for you are with me;
your rod and your staff,
they comfort me.
You prepare a table before me
in the presence of my enemies.
You anoint my head with oil;
my cup overflows.
Surely your goodness and love will follow me
all the days of my life,
and I will dwell in the house of the LORD
forever.

21

Cultivate Gentleness

Thaw with her gentle persuasion is more
powerful than Thor with his hammer.
The one melts, the other breaks into pieces.

—HENRY DAVID THOREAU

Aesop, the legendary author of fables, gave us this little story about gentleness:

The North Wind and the Sun quarreled about which of them was the stronger. While disputing with much heat and bluster, a traveler passed along the road wrapped in a cloak. "Let us agree," said the Sun, "that he is the stronger who can strip that traveler of his cloak." "Very well," growled the North Wind, and sent a cold, howling blast against the traveler.

With the first gust of wind the ends of the cloak whipped about the traveler's body. But he immediately wrapped it closely around him, and the harder the wind blew, the tighter he held it to him. The North Wind tore angrily at the cloak, but all his efforts were in vain.

Then the Sun began to shine. At first his beams were gentle, and in the pleasant warmth after the bitter cold of the North Wind, the traveler unfastened his cloak and let it hang loosely from his shoulders. The Sun's rays grew warmer. The traveler took off his cap and mopped his brow. He became so heated that he pulled off his cloak, and, to escape the blazing sunshine, threw himself down in the welcome shade of a tree by the roadside.

There's a lesson in this brief tale: gentleness and kind persuasion win where force and bluster fail.

22

Examine Your Faith

Faith is an oasis in the heart which will never
be reached by the caravan of thinking.

—KAHLIL GIBRAN

We often wrestle with questions we can't answer: What caused life to begin? How were the laws of nature established? How can every human being have a unique DNA code?

Questions about our faith that we can't answer can have us questioning our personal beliefs and cause a considerable amount of unrest. But faith is more than just a belief. A belief often relates to the past—a belief about what already happened. At its core, however, faith is a deeply rooted expectation of all the good things to come—what will happen. Faith goes beyond belief and reaches far into the future. Good or bad, it's what you trust will happen.

When contentment is lacking, often it's because faith is lacking. What we feel in the present has very little to do with the past, and more with how we feel—or in this case, expect—the future will go. If we expect the future to go well, we feel content. If we expect the future to be bleak, we succumb to worry and discontent.

Examine your faith today by answering these questions:

1. What is one thing you believe will happen in the future with absolute certainty—something that causes you discontent?
2. Why do you believe it? Do you know for sure that it's true?
3. In what or whom do you anchor your trust?

4. What is one action you could take to build faith—and expect the best as a result—and begin to cultivate contentment in this area?

But faith is more than just a belief. A Christian's faith is rooted in a relationship with Jesus. When we recognize Him as our Savior and Lord, we can more easily accept that we won't always know or understand everything we want to know and understand. Besides, how could we finite human beings with our finite minds ever grasp all that our infinite God is about?

We can, though, know God—His goodness, faithfulness, power, and love. Because of God's immeasurable love, we can expect Him to be with us, whatever we are currently experiencing and whatever we will encounter in the future.

Often when we are low on contentment, we are low on faith. We may also be trusting more in our feelings than in what we know about God. If we focus on Him instead of on our circumstances, we can find reassurance as well as contentment in His love.

What is just one fact about God that helps you have hope for the future? What will you do today to strengthen your faith?

23

Trust the God Behind the Absolutes

Faith is not a one-and-done transaction. Faith in Jesus is a relationship that—like any relationship—needs to be nurtured consistently. We invest in our relationship with Jesus one day at a time. Living in relationship with Him helps us stand strong against doubt, fear, worry, and the enemy's lies.

Consider, too, evidence of God's faithfulness in the world around you. The sun rises and sets every day. The same constellations appear in the sky. Seasons come regularly, one after the other. The law of gravity has never wavered. What examples of God's faithfulness to you personally can you add to the list? Practice rooting your faith in God in personal evidence as well as big-picture evidence of His faithfulness.

Also look for goodness all around you—and for opportunities to be good to others. Whose kind and caring actions of others have blessed you? To whom will you be kind and caring today? Our choice to give can increase our contentment as much as receiving can.

When your faith dwindles, turn your thoughts to God; remind yourself of His role as the Sustainer of life and the Author of history. Trust the God behind the absolutes.

24

Appreciate the Little Joys

That man is rich whose pleasures are the cheapest.

—HENRY DAVID THOREAU

We can find contentment in the simplest of things. All around us and every day, life is filled with little joys. If we're always in a hurry, though, we might not see them.

Make a conscious effort to embrace joy-filled moments like these:

- Sharing a long, savory supper with a loved one on a crisp fall evening.
- Sipping your morning coffee as you watch the sun rise.
- Wrapping yourself in a warm, fluffy bath towel after a long, hot shower.
- Snuggling with your dog or cat as you sit on the sofa.
- Hearing your daughter's giggles when she plays.
- Seeing your son's enormous smile when he learns something new.
- Welcoming winter's first snowfall.
- Celebrating spring's first flowers.
- Enjoying a gentle breeze on a warm summer day.
- Marveling at autumn's brilliant colors.
- Experiencing the comfort that comes with holding a loved one's hand.

Open your eyes today to all the simple joys of life.

25

Simplify

He is rich who is content with the least;
for contentment is the wealth of nature.

—SOCRATES

Let's face it. It's difficult to be content when dishes and laundry have piled up, the kids' toys are scattered throughout the house, your dresser drawers are so full they won't close, and your closet flat-out refuses to allow you to put another item inside.

Then come other tasks: Papers to file. Mail to open. Dog hair to vacuum up. Missing socks to find and pair with their mates. Books to sort through so newer ones fit in the bookcase. Two thousand email messages to read.

Life can be overwhelming, can't it? With all these tasks and many more, how can you even concentrate? Sometimes simplifying is what's needed to bring contentment.

Declutter. Keep only what you need. Reduce the number of voices calling for your attention.

Which aspect of your life feels the most cluttered? The most overstuffed? Where might you incorporate the "less is more" principle? It could be a room in your home, a dusty collection of tchotchkes, an unworkable relationship or two, your car, your closet, your desktop, or your sock drawer.

Start where you are. Look around. You might choose the area in your home that most needs attention or tackle what's literally right in front of you. Would that be a messy desk? A cluttered table? A dirty floor? Start with what you see. Tidy up a bit.

And breathe.

26
Connect with Your Contentment

I would maintain that thanks are the highest
form of thought; and that gratitude is
happiness doubled by wonder.

—G. K. CHESTERTON

When do you feel most content? Could it be that some feelings of contentment were so fleeting that you've forgotten them?

Keeping a gratitude journal is one way of remembering these special moments. If you allow yourself just five minutes a day to write in a journal, to list a few of the day's little joys, you will become more aware of the richness of your life and of God's great goodness to you. How you choose to journal is up to you. Be creative. You can write in a print journal or keep a list on your smartphone. You can make bulleted lists, write out sentences or paragraphs, include thank-you notes to God and others, or even create a photo journal.

Dig deeper into your thoughts, being sure to capture details. The repetitiveness of generalities can lead to boredom, so use details that come from your heart. Compare these two statements and see which one generates more gratitude and contentment in you:

1. I am grateful for my husband.
2. I am grateful for my husband making a delicious dinner last night when he knew I was tired. I could even smell the fresh herbs!

Use adjectives to describe the object for which you are grateful and your specific feelings. Now compare these two statements and notice which one lights you up when you read it:

1. I am grateful for my husband.
2. I am grateful for my romantic husband whose little surprises fill me up with joy. Yesterday he left a love note in my purse, and today he surprised me by taking me out on a dinner date!

Search for contentment in relationships past and present. Find contentment in the kind acts of others. Think about different aspects of your life: What are you most grateful for at work? What obstacles in your life have you overcome? Which are the best traits you inherited from earlier generations of your family?

On challenging days, open your gratitude journal and shift your attention to what is positive. By journaling, you learn not only to notice little moments of contentment, but also to grab on to them and cherish them.

27

Displace Discontent

Remember, as it was written, to love another
person is to see the face of God.

—VICTOR HUGO

Sometimes it's good to notice discontent. The kind that is akin to discomfort can drive us to act and move us forward toward something better. Discontentment works much like pain in the body: each is a messenger that indicates something might be wrong.

Discontent can also rob us of love. Paul wrote about love in 1 Corinthians 13:4–7. There he described what love *isn't*. He said love *isn't* jealous, arrogant, proud, rude, or selfish. It doesn't get upset with others or keep count of wrongs. When we work against love, then our hearts can't be content. And in this vicious cycle, our discontent—our dissatisfaction and unhappiness—can have us working against love either consciously or unconsciously. And working against love further fuels our discontent.

Stop for a moment and examine your heart. Has any jealousy, arrogance, pride, rudeness, or selfishness slipped in unnoticed? Awareness of those love blockers is the first step toward getting rid of them. Ask God to show you the roots of your jealousy or to help you understand why you are too often rude to others. Ask Him, too, to help you displace those attitudes and behaviors with His kind of love, with love that rejoices over the truth, always trusts, always hopes, and lasts forever.

28

Beware the Green-Eyed Monster

Comparison is the thief of joy.

—THEODORE ROOSEVELT

Envy, the first love blocker listed, comes when we compare ourselves with others: "*She* has a great job, a perfect husband, well-behaved children, an awesome house, money for fancy clothes and trips—and *why don't I?*"

In the story of Othello, Shakespeare wrote, "Oh, beware, my lord, of jealousy! It is the green-eyed monster." And this monster keeps us from knowing contentment. It also turns love toward indifference. Worst of all, our envy says to God, "What You've provided for me is not good enough."

Stop envy before it takes root. Sometimes visualization can help you do exactly that. Think about David and Goliath in 1 Samuel 17. Young David used just a sling and a stone to knock down and defeat the huge Philistine warrior. So imagine yourself as David and picture Goliath as the green-eyed monster. Whenever envy threatens you, knock it down! Turn your thoughts toward gratitude. Choose to be thankful for what you have.

Realize, too, that you may not actually want what she has because you don't know *all* that she has or what *she* may be dealing with. Remember that the grass may *look* greener, but each person is fighting her own battles.

Again, the next time you find yourself making comparisons or battling envy, notice what you already have in your own life. Who knew your own grass could look so green!

29

Free Yourself from Envy

Envy is a gun with a faulty breech-lock which
flares back and burns the gunner.

—AUSTIN O'MALLEY

Envy is defined by *Merriam-Webster* as "painful or resentful awareness of an advantage enjoyed by another joined with a desire to possess the same advantage." No wonder envy can propel you into a cyclone of negative emotions: disappointment, depression, anger, guilt, shame, and even hatred.

When envy creeps in, arrest it by trying some exercises in generosity.

- Volunteer. Focus on others.
- Be generous. Give something away. Meet a need.
- Tell someone you're grateful for them.

Then enjoy being free—or at least freer—of envy, and watch miracles take place in your life.

Don't forget to be generous with yourself. Look inward and appreciate your own growth. If experiencing envy, while looking inward ask yourself, "What is it that I *really* want?" Then make a list. This information provides the important lesson that some good can come from envy. Specifically, our envy can lead to self-improvement.

When you stop chasing other people's dreams and begin chasing your own, you can make positive changes in your life and can move toward those things you truly desire.

30

Give Away the Glory

It was pride that changed angels into devils;
it is humility that makes men as angels.

—SAINT AUGUSTINE

Aesop had a way with using fables as teaching tools. Have you heard the story about the rooster and the eagle?

Once there were two roosters living in the same farmyard who could not bear the sight of each other. At last one day they decided to fight it out, beak and claw. They fought until one of them was beaten and crawled off into a corner to hide. The rooster that won the battle flew to the top of the henhouse and, proudly flapping his wings, crowed with all his might to tell the world about his victory. But an eagle, circling overhead, heard the boasting chanticleer, swooped down, and carried the rooster away. When his rival saw what had happened, he came out of his corner and took his place as master of the farmyard.

Here is the moral to Aesop's fable: *Pride goes before a fall.*

Pride is another of those contentment-draining love blockers Paul warned about. First, know there is a difference between being prideful and being proud. Prideful people think of themselves as better than others. The word *arrogant* comes to mind. To be proud, on the other hand, is to be pleased with something you, a family member, or a friend has achieved often due to hard work and commitment. Humility is vital to this kind of celebratory pride. Maybe you have observed someone proudly, gratefully accept an award and then give God or someone else in their life credit for the achievement.

Think about all the great things you have accomplished in your life. When you've celebrated your achievements, have you given credit to the others who deserved acknowledgment? Have you had any mentors help you along? What about a teacher who believed in you? Or a spouse who handles everything in the home so you can follow your dreams?

Take a few minutes right now to think about all the people in your life who have helped you accomplish those things you're most proud of. As a bonus, let each person know how much you appreciate them for who they are or the difference they've made in your life. When you send the note or email or text, you'll be blessed by the surge of contentment that fills your heart.

31

Extend grace

Grace is the face that love wears when it meets imperfection.

—JOSEPH R. COOKE

The world was a kinder place when people interacted face-to-face. It isn't easy to say rude things when you're looking someone in the eyes. Slamming someone over social media or with a flippant text message is much easier—and that is happening far too much. Freedom of speech has lost its filter. Thoughtless, disrespectful, hurtful comments run rampant today in social media, late-night talk shows, and even the news.

How do you deal with rude people? When someone is rude to you, maybe your first reaction is to be rude right back. Rudeness responding to rudeness destroys peace. There are better ways to deal with a person's lack of courtesy and kindness.

Recognize that someone's imperfections are just that. If a person makes a disagreeable comment on your social media post, cuts in front of you in the grocery line, or, ignoring you, keeps talking on their cell phone, don't take it personally. Their behavior is about them, not you. So rather than allowing something to upset you and steal your contentment, practice grace by taking the following steps:

1. Take a deep breath.
2. Remember what you're committed to in your heart.
3. Lead by example and treat them the way you would like to be treated.

4. Go one step further and offer authentic listening, an act of kindness, or help with something you learn they are dealing with.

Extending grace to difficult people takes practice, but remembering how many times you have received grace makes extending it to others a little easier. Blessing people with grace—with the grace of mercy, kindness, humility, gentleness, or patience—can help break the cycle of upset in the world. Become a beacon of grace and peace.

Grace
is the face
that love
wears

32

Be a Light for Others

We make a living by what we get. But
we make a life by what we give.

—WINSTON CHURCHILL

Selfishness is another love blocker that pulls us further away from unity and community. The cure for selfishness is to stop living only for yourself and extend generosity to the world. When you set selfishness aside and instead focus on the needs of others, you make the world a better place, your light shines brightly, and you experience a rich sense of contentment.

The generosity you extend can have many different faces. You can be generous with your money, yes. But you can also be generous with your time and your listening. Take time to talk to your family members, friends, and others. Find out what is important to them. Stay connected. Have fun. Being generous with your time and attention results in stronger relationships.

You can also be generous with your space by giving others the space they need, both physical space and space to grow emotionally and spiritually. With our children, for instance, this kind of generosity may mean taking a step back and allowing them more freedom. If you are physically strong, you can be generous with your strength and help people with projects that require heavy lifting. And if you are strong emotionally, you can be generous with your listening skills and support.

Examine your strengths, skills, and talents. Think beyond what's material. Then make a specific plan to be generous. You'll be a light in someone's life.

33

Make Your Love Stronger

Every sixty seconds you spend upset is a minute
of happiness you'll never get back.

—UNKNOWN

Whether you are dating or have been married for years, the little but upsetting things your significant other does can pile up in a mound of discontent, and love can get lost in the heap. Instead of allowing that to happen, focus on the good things about your partner, those special traits that make you feel loved, those commitments that earn your respect, those skills that simplify your life. Choose your battles and let go of those things that, in the big picture of life, are too petty to mention. And when something upsetting *does* need to be addressed, do so with the patience and kindness that characterize love, not with jealousy, arrogance, or pride.

Relationships are a journey, and every journey has its ups and downs. Know that love and grace can keep you moving forward. Try the following exercise:

- Make a list of what you love about your significant other or spouse.
- What do you love about the way he or she looks or acts?
- What actions and accomplishments make you proud of him or her?
- In what ways do you wish you were more like this person?

Great! Now let this special person know what you love and what makes you proud of him or her! I'm not sure whose heart will be more content after sharing.

What are you trying to teach me?

34

Lean In

> You will never be happy if you continue to search
> for what happiness consists of. You will never live
> if you are looking for the meaning of life.
>
> —ALBERT CAMUS

In what aspects of your life are you not content *at all*? When you struggle with a deep discontent, it's normal to want to avoid any of those situations causing the unhappiness and ignore your feelings. But maybe you've heard the phrase "Whatever you resist persists."

That said, what do you think would happen if you leaned in to discontent and discomfort just a bit? This isn't the same as giving in or giving up. I'm just suggesting that you consider what it might be trying to teach you. If you resist it, you'll never hear, much less learn, that lesson.

When discontent arises, try the following:

1. Close your eyes. Imagine your discontent is sitting there with you. What color, shape, and size is it? Or—maybe—where is it located in your body? Does it move?
2. Ask your discontent—and God—"What are you trying to teach me?"
3. Wait for a moment and listen.
4. Write down your thoughts and discover for yourself what action steps you can take to address it.

Reasons for being discontent vary, but occasionally feeling discontent is normal. It only becomes a problem when it rules your life.

35

Live in the Moment

Live in the present, launch yourself at every
wave, find eternity in each moment.

—HENRY DAVID THOREAU

Contentment comes from learning to live day by day, hour by hour, moment by moment, and it comes as we learn to stay in the present. Neither straying back to yesterday, wishing the past were different, nor peeking into tomorrow, worrying about the future, will bring us contentment. Focusing on the present moment—on the right now—can.

And focusing now.

And now.

And now.

Notice how each now is different from the last.

Notice the air around you.

Notice the sounds.

Notice the smells.

Notice the colors and textures.

Notice any people or animals.

Learning to be present brings you peace in the moment, moving you closer to true contentment, making you aware that you aren't traveling life's path alone and there's hope for the future.

Start right now practicing living with just today in mind. Then live with just this hour in mind. Soon you will savor these God-given moments and notice the richness and abundance of blessings that is already here for you.

Also, address problems when they come up; don't allow them to follow you into tomorrow. Celebrate every challenge you overcome. Open your eyes and choose to appreciate the little things, all those wonderful, comforting blessings that bring you joy. And remember, you only get to live today once—so make today a good one!

LIVE
in this
PERFECT
moment

36
Make Things Less Complicated

Today is a good day to have a good day.

—UNKNOWN

We make many aspects of life so complicated, don't we?

Below is a lovely little reminder to stop doing that. The following has been adapted from the wise words of Dr. Frank Crane, a columnist for the *Boston Globe*, who penned these words in 1921.

Just for Today . . .

I will try to live through this day only, and not tackle my whole life-problem at once.

I will be happy. Happiness is from within; it is not a matter of externals.

I will adjust myself to what is and not try to adjust everything to my own desires.

I will take care of my body. I will exercise it, care for it, nourish it, and not abuse or neglect it.

I will try to strengthen my mind. I will study. I will learn something useful. I will read something that requires effort, thought, and concentration.

I will exercise my soul in three ways:

I will do somebody a good turn and not get found out.

I will do at least two things I don't want to do.

Just for today, I will not show anyone that my feelings are hurt.

I will be agreeable. I will look as well as I can, dress as becomingly as possible, talk low, act courteously, be liberal with flattery, criticize not one bit nor find fault with anything, and not try to regulate or improve anybody.

I will have a program. I will write down just what I expect to do. I may not follow it exactly, but I'll have it. It will save me from hurry, indecision, and discontent.

I will have a quiet half hour, all by myself, to relax. During this half hour I will talk with God to get a better perspective on my life.

Just for today, I will be unafraid. Especially I will not be afraid to be happy, to enjoy what is beautiful, to love and to believe that those I love, love me.

Just for today, I will be happy.

37

Use Your Talents

Every natural power exhilarates; a true
talent delights the possessor first.

—RALPH WALDO EMERSON

You have God-given passions, skills, and talents—things you do well naturally—and you've put hundreds or thousands of hours of practice into others. Along with skill comes confidence. When you put these talents and skills to use each day, you will find both your confidence and therefore your contentment increasing. And sharing your gifts with others can move you even closer to that place of being truly content.

Also, because we each have different gifts, amazing things can happen when we bring them together. For example, each musician in an orchestra brings a certain skill, and when these talented, practiced individuals combine their skills, they make beautiful music. People bringing together their unique abilities happens in communities and companies every day, and what results are innovative technologies, films, art, fashion, cuisine, new city planning—and so much more.

Take time today to make an inventory and list *all* the things in life that you do well. Which items on your list come to you naturally? Into which have you invested countless hours to hone your skills? Which bring you the greatest delight? What skills have you not used for a while? Which of your skills would you most like to share with others?

Your special abilities might bless others and contribute to someone else's contentment. In fact, the gifts you share today could even change someone's life forever.

38

Serve Others

The essence of life is to serve others and do good.

—ARISTOTLE

We all have the ability to serve in some way. Even with a physical limitation, we can serve by reading aloud to others, by sending a note of encouragement, by using our minds to solve a problem, by being still in prayer and meditation. We can simply smile. We can serve in ways that are simple or complex, done alone or with others.

If you're not sure where you'd like to serve on your own, serve with others. Serving together is a rewarding and memorable way to spend time with family and friends. Today, make a plan to do something together in service. Decide how your combined gifts can work collectively to meet a need. It can be as simple as cooking a meal for someone who is dealing with a challenging life event, or it can be something that takes more work and planning, like a fundraiser, for example.

In the Bible, Job's friend Elihu said that people who serve God "will spend the rest of their days in prosperity and their years in contentment" (Job 36:11). When you serve others, you will become rich in God's blessings and experience a kind of contentment that money can't buy.

39

Lend a Helping Hand

Only a life lived in the service to others is worth living.

—ALBERT EINSTEIN

Still not sure where to lend a helping hand? May one of the following ideas stir your heart and help you begin serving on your own or with others:

- Collect household and food items for a family in need.
- Volunteer at a local homeless shelter or animal shelter.
- Donate food to a local food bank.
- Walk a neighbor's pet.
- Donate school supplies to a school or toys to a childcare center.
- Share a skill or talent you have by teaching classes.
- Organize a clothing drive for the local homeless shelter.
- Adopt and tidy up a public part of your neighborhood.
- Plant trees or flowers for everyone to see and enjoy.
- Make a garden for yourself—and give away your harvest.
- Volunteer at a local library.
- Donate electronics to a school or homeless shelter.
- Take stuffed animals to children in hospitals.
- Foster a dog or cat in your home.
- Use your crafting skills to brighten someone's day.
- Take flowers or little gifts to nursing home residents.
- Send thank-you cards to local police departments and fire stations.

40

Teach Someone

A teacher affects eternity; he can never
tell where his influence stops.

—HENRY ADAMS

Teachers have a profound influence on our lives. Maybe there was one teacher in particular who helped shape your life.

As a spouse, parent, companion, or friend, you are a teacher too. Whether intentionally or not, you have likely taught someone to do something. To you, that action might have been small, but you opened up a world of new possibilities for the other person. Think about a time when you saw the positive effect of your teaching. It was a moment of rich contentment, wasn't it?

If you teach a child to ride a bike, you start them on the path to freedom. If you teach a friend to play an instrument, you add more music to the world. And if you teach someone about God, that truth can change their life forever!

Take time to share your gifts and your knowledge. What will you teach someone today?

41
Show and Tell

Children learn more from what you
are, than what you teach.

—W. E. B. DU BOIS

Have you thought about the fact that, beginning today, you can guide the young people in your life toward contentment? Now is the best time to guide little ones into a future where they feel safe and confident—but it's never too late. Know that much of your guidance will be your example and practices rather than your words.

Think of all the children and young people in your life, whether or not they're related to you. Then read through these ideas for how to introduce them to a life of contentment:

1. Volunteer together at an organization *they* care about and show them that they can already make a difference in the world.
2. One in, one out. During special times when they receive gifts, such as birthdays or holidays, let children choose those personal belongings that they would like to donate to others less fortunate. Doing so teaches abundance and trust that they will always have what they truly need.
3. Create a wish list. Have young people write about or make a collage of pictures that show what they'd love to have or create in their lives. Then discuss what it takes to build that future. Coming up with plans creates confidence.

4. Give thanks. At mealtimes, ask your children what they are grateful for today. Then thank God together.
5. Celebrate! Every victory deserves to be acknowledged. Not only will the celebration boost their confidence, but it will be a good opportunity for you to tell them how amazing they are and make them feel special!

Help young ones learn the joy of giving. Be an example. Show children how you incorporate ways to give into your daily life. Talk about what you do, why you do it, and the contentment and joy you experience.

Spoiler alert: As you watch these children grow in contentment, you just might discover that your contentment is growing too!

42

Be an Encourager

A word of encouragement during a failure
is worth more than an hour of praise after success.

—UNKNOWN

Some people seem to be born with the gift of encouragement. If that's you, then you have probably already seen the power of your words and how they can turn someone's day around. It's also likely that you have a heart for others and are a terrific listener.

If encouragement *doesn't* come easily to you, don't worry!

Again, let me reassure you that you don't have to be born an encourager. Building up and affirming people is a skill you can learn and sharpen. Below are three steps you can take toward becoming a world-class encourager:

1. Look around you. What are the people in your life talking about? What concerns or worries do they have? Ask them how you can help. Better yet, make a specific offer if you have an idea. Oftentimes, this question or offer alone is encouraging. We all like to know that someone cares.

2. Make someone's day by letting that person know how much she means to you. Remind her of her strengths or tell her something you like about her. Who doesn't want to hear a statement like that?

3. Show up. Oftentimes your physical presence is encouragement enough. Your being there says something to the people in your

life—without even saying a word! If you're not one to encourage with words, realize that the simple act of showing up for the people in your life speaks volumes. Dinner, celebrations, weddings, funerals, kids' sporting events—being present at occasions like these demonstrates to the people you love that they matter to you.

43

go World-Class

Our chief want is someone who will inspire
us to be what we know we could be.

—RALPH WALDO EMERSON

If you already practice encouragement, let's take you to the next level: world-class encourager. Can you imagine if you had this type of encourager in your own life, championing you? It starts with you!

- Send a note. Speaking words of encouragement is wonderful. Taking the time to write them down on paper (bonus points if you use pretty stationery) is next-level.
- Each time you introduce someone—whether your spouse, a friend, or a colleague—include a word or phrase of authentic praise. The more specific you are, the greater the encouragement will be.
- Go global. Our social media feeds are full of discouragement and divisiveness. What if you decided only to post words that encourage, inspire, educate, and elevate?
- When you receive exemplary service, write a note to the employee's supervisor. You might just get that person promoted and make a difference for their whole family.

The gift of encouraging people just takes a bit of intentionality and practice, but as you grow in your ability to offer encouragement, watch your own life light up!

FALL SEVEN TIMES, STAND UP EIGHT

44

Don't Quit

Fall seven times, stand up eight.

—JAPANESE PROVERB

If you know someone who needs a little encouragement during a difficult time, this abridged poem by Edgar Guest is perfect for sharing.

KEEP GOING

When things go wrong, as they sometimes will,
And the road you're trudging seems all uphill,
When care is pressing you down a bit,
Rest if you must—but don't you quit!
Life is strange with its twists and turns,
As every one of us sometimes learns.
Don't give up though the pace seems slow—
You may succeed with another blow.
Often the goal is nearer than
It seems to a faint and faltering man.
Often the struggler has given up
When he might have captured the victor's cup;
And he learned too late when the night slipped down,
How close he was to the golden crown.
And you can never tell how close you are
It may be near when it seems afar.
So stick to the fight when you're hardest hit—
It's when things seem worst that you mustn't quit.

45

Practice the Art of Giving

If you have much, give of your wealth;
if you have little, give of your heart.

—UNKNOWN

Just as some people are natural encouragers, other people are natural giv-ers. They don't even have to think about it. And *giving* doesn't necessarily mean giving money. Oh, it's good to give to your church or favorite charities. Financial support is essential to these organizations that matter to you, but just as important is the giving of yourself.

The gifts of your time, presence, patience, and care are like gold to the recipient. The gift of *you* is what others will remember long after a gift of cash. Giving yourself strengthens your bond with others, and that richer connec-tion means happiness and contentment for you and the people around you.

Today, think about ways you can give more of yourself to your family, your friends, your church, your neighbors, and your community.

46

Give Cheerfully

> The wise man does not lay up his own treasures. The
> more he gives to others, the more he has for his own.
>
> —LAO TZU

There's giving out of obligation, and then there's giving *cheerfully*. Giving
generously. Giving just because.

Doesn't it add to your contentment when you write a sweet note and
tuck it into your child's backpack or your husband's lunch sack? Do you feel
happy when you're planning a small surprise for a coworker or neighbor? Acts
of giving—and little acts definitely count!—result in contentment not only
for the recipient but also for the giver.

Here are several ways to give that you might not have thought of:

- Give the gift of heritage to your children by researching and
  creating a family tree.
- Be aware of elderly, single neighbors who are alone on holidays. Give
  them the gift of celebration by inviting them for a meal or dessert.
- Donate blood at your local blood bank.
- Drop off an unopened bag of kibble to your local animal shelter.
- Give to those who give! Write thank-you notes or take treats to
  volunteers in your school, church, or community.

Whatever you give, do so with a solid dose of your cheerfulness and joy!

47

Use Your Leadership

I must follow the people. Am I not their leader?

—BENJAMIN DISRAELI

In 1995, leadership expert Sally Helgesen published a study of female leaders and their leadership styles in her book, *The Female Advantage: Women's Ways of Leadership*. She discovered five key ways women excel as leaders:

1. Women value relationships.
2. They prefer direct communication.
3. Women are comfortable with diversity.
4. They put themselves at the center of those groups they lead.
5. They are skilled at integrating their personal lives with their work lives.

Supporting these assertions is a 2015 Gallup poll showing that female leaders are more engaged with their counterparts than male leaders. The poll found women better at building relationships with their subordinates, encouraging a positive team environment and providing employees with opportunities to develop their careers.

But leadership is needed beyond the workplace, and many women are born with the ability to lead. Day by day, they use their God-given relationship building and multitasking skills at home, in the church, and throughout their communities. As they use their leadership gifts, these women grow in strength, and the tangible results of their leadership add to their overall feelings of contentment.

Are you a leader? Maybe you think of yourself as an introvert, a little shy, and more of a follower. Read again the five points listed. Do you see any or all of these traits in yourself? You might be a leader and not even know it!

Never underestimate your ability to lead and influence. Consider both how to sharpen your leadership skills and ways to use them each day. Then lead in a way that guides others toward contentment.

48

Have Mercy

I have always found that mercy bears
richer fruits than strict justice.

—ABRAHAM LINCOLN

Do you find it easy to be tenderhearted toward others? Are you able to show kindness to those you feel don't deserve it?

Answering yes to either or both of those questions suggests you have the gift of mercy, and that gift can be a lifeline for those people who are struggling. And mercy is always there and ready today if you want to share it. You can choose to share it now, later, or never. You can even allow mercy to lie dormant.

But I hope you don't choose that last option because mercy is one of the greatest gifts you can give someone. Mercy allows you to express compassion and understanding. It recognizes that hurt often underlies anger; that kindness can trump hatred, fear, and even ignorance; and that forgiveness can soften hard hearts and heal broken hearts. Mercy is acting in response to the deep love God has for you and extending His love to others.

Learning to be merciful and making mercy part of your everyday life leads to that comfortable place of true contentment—that place where even when things don't feel okay, they are okay because God is right there in the middle of it all.

Is there someone who needs a little mercy from you today? Think about it. Don't let that gift of mercy gather dust in your heart.

Sweet mercy
is nobility's
true badge

49

Add Joy to Sweet Mercy

Sweet mercy is nobility's true badge.

—WILLIAM SHAKESPEARE

As you've seen with many of these Christlike traits, there is always a deeper level. So think of living out these traits as an art to be practiced and mastered. When it comes to mercy, there is extending mercy, and then there's extending *sweet* mercy—joyfully.

Sometimes, however, the best we can do is simply have mercy in our hearts, and that is truly a great place to start. After all, in some circumstances face-to-face mercy isn't possible. It could even be unsafe or unhealthy. We're not talking about those times.

We're talking about the more everyday opportunities when we have the ability to extend mercy. Adding sweetness and joy, when possible, makes for a completely different experience for both the receiver of mercy and the giver—you. A generous act of mercy allows space for healing and transformation to take place. The person receiving sweet mercy may feel a sense of freedom, relief, appreciation, love, and so much more.

You can show sweet mercy by, for instance, truly forgiving others, giving unselfishly to those in need, praying for those who have hurt you, meeting rudeness with kindness, speaking kindly of others, and learning to love others just as they are. Add to this list being merciful to yourself. When you learn to forgive and be kind to yourself, you'll find it easier to extend mercy to others—and to do so joyfully. And joyfully extending sweet mercy definitely leads you closer to contentment.

50

Let the Future Pull You Forward

The best way to predict your future is to create it.

—ABRAHAM LINCOLN

It isn't wrong to make plans or look to the future, but it's important not to get too caught up in it. And it may not be helpful to compare where you are today with where you want to be. When the goal seems unreachable, remember that things change. Unimaginable things—good as well as bad—happen. Steadily committing to a day-by-day process will lead you to the incredible future you desire.

Our rapidly advancing technology offers us an example. A little more than a century ago, if you had said that astronauts would walk on the moon, few people would have believed you. Back then, the Wright brothers were trying to make their wooden aircraft get off the ground. Could Alexander Graham Bell have imagined us talking to others, face-to-face, on tiny phones that fit in our purses, our pockets, and the palms of our hands?

Yet new tools have been built, and new technology developed. New inventions exist today because of the perseverance and the daily research, experiments, and studies that people before us were committed to. They had a vision—some that would become reality only way off in the future—but they had to embrace their daily tasks in order to make progress toward ultimately fulfilling that vision.

Each day comes with its own celebrations, its own failures, and everything in between. We needn't worry about tomorrow. But if you have a vision for the future that is calling you forward, what is one step you can take today to move closer to having that vision become reality? May your heart be content as you move another step into your future.

EVERY DAY is the best DAY

51

Approach Every Day as the Best Day

Apparently there is nothing that cannot happen today.

—MARK TWAIN

Each day is the gift of a new beginning. We don't know what a new day will hold, and what happens each day isn't always in our control. But how we respond is always in our control.

Read what the great essayist, philosopher, and poet Ralph Waldo Emerson had to say about embracing each new day.

Write it on your heart
that every day is the best day in the year.
He is rich who owns the day, and no one owns the day
who allows it to be invaded with fret and anxiety.
Finish every day and be done with it.
You have done what you could.
Some blunders and absurdities, no doubt crept in.
Forget them as soon as you can, tomorrow is a new day;
begin it well and serenely, with too high a spirit
to be cumbered with your old nonsense.
This new day is too dear,
with its hopes and invitations,
to waste a moment on the yesterdays.

"Forever is composed of nows."

EMILY DICKINSON

52

Notice the Now

Forever is composed of nows.

—EMILY DICKINSON

How well do you live in the moment? Be brutally honest with yourself. Take *this* moment right now and really look at how you spend your days. Do you often stroll down memory lane? Or are you worried about something that *might* happen in the future?

Finding contentment relies on being rooted in the present. Just as an anchor holds a ship in place, the present holds you safely right where you are—unless you decide to haul in that anchor and sail to the past or the future, where all kinds of storms can upset your otherwise calm sea.

Let's try an experiment. What has been troubling you most? Is it a memory of something you wish had never happened? That's simply the past. Or are you worried and stressed about something that may happen . . . in the future, near or far? However troubling either the event you remember or the event you anticipate may be, those events are not happening *now*.

This moment—this now—is all you have. And all you will ever have. When you begin to notice with your senses all the things around you, your experience of life will become calmer, richer, and more full of joy and gratitude.

Taking five minutes each day to notice the now can help remind us of what we can do when we begin to worry or feel stress. In any given moment, you can stop and notice the now. Suddenly you'll discover a little more space for living fully in the moment, which more often than not is quite content.

53

Be Wise About Your Wants

Where sense is wanting, everything is wanting.

—BENJAMIN FRANKLIN

Have you heard the fable by Aesop about the dog and his bone?

A dog, to whom the butcher had thrown a bone, was hurrying home with his prize as fast as he could go. As he crossed a narrow footbridge, he happened to look down and saw himself reflected in the quiet water as if in a mirror. But the desirous dog thought he saw a real dog carrying a bone much bigger than his own. If he had stopped to think, he would have known better. But instead of thinking, he dropped his bone and sprang at the dog in the river only to find himself swimming for dear life to reach the shore. At last he managed to scramble out, and as he stood sadly thinking about the good bone he had lost, he realized what an unwise dog he had been.

What about you? Are you a wise or unwise dog? Do you have enough, or do you want more?

It isn't wrong to want more, but when you're *always* wanting more, you may want to figure out why. After all, wanting more interferes with being content in life. Feelings of contentment and feelings of lack don't buddy up so well, so be wise about your wanting.

Contentment comes when your wants are authentic, from the heart, even when you don't have what you want just yet. It comes when you have a plan to get what you authentically want—not what you think you *should* have and not those things you say you want when you are simply comparing. Those things may be nice to have, but they will never fulfill you.

Make a list of what you *truly* want. List things both big and small. Put a star next to the most important wants. Pick one, maybe the one that you can achieve the soonest. Now make a list of five things you can do to make this want into something you have. When you see the gap begin to close and know that having this want is only a matter of time, contentment quickly follows.

54

Realize You Have Everything You Need

If you have a garden and a library,
you have everything you need!

—MARCUS TULLIUS CICERO

Whether or not you have your own garden or a library nearby, you likely have everything you need—I mean *actually* need—in order to survive.

If you are reading this book—though I don't want to make assumptions—you likely have the following: a functioning brain, air in your lungs, clean water, enough food to sustain you, a place to lay your head, and access to God's creation.

If you're even more blessed, you have a place to call home, a community, a job, family, and friends.

Beyond that, according to a 2016 headline from *Forbes*, "If You Have $10 and No Debt, You Are Richer Than 25% of America."

How's *that* for perspective?

When you think about all the things you don't have compared to all that you *do* have, you just may see that . . .

You actually do have everything you need. And more.

55

Sing a New Song

He who sings frightens away his ills.

—MIGUEL DE CERVANTES

In 1938 British missionary Gladys Aylward found herself in the middle of a crisis while she was serving in China. She was caring for a hundred orphans when the region was invaded by Communist Japanese forces. Gladys and the children were forced to flee on foot through the mountains. Their goal was to find safety in Siam, more than 250 miles away. On the twelfth day of walking, they arrived at the Yellow River, but they couldn't cross. The Chinese army had hidden the boats to keep them from getting into the hands of the Japanese. Gladys was tired, worn, and at a loss about what to do.

"Why don't we cross?" the children asked.

"There are no boats," Gladys answered.

Then one of the children said, "God can do anything. Let's ask Him to get us across."

So they knelt, prayed, and sang. A Chinese soldier was nearby, and he heard their singing. He brought a boat so they could cross safely and continue their journey to Siam.

Maybe there is something you desperately want or need. You have prayed about it, but still you are no nearer to what you want or need. Perhaps you find discontent welling up inside you as your faith dwindles. Like Gladys on the riverbank, you are at a loss about what to do.

Think of a song that you find uplifting. A song of gratitude and praise. (If you don't know one, make one up!) You see, research shows that music affects your mood, and singing has been shown to improve mental health and well-being. Don't believe me? Try it.

A grateful heart—fueled by your choice to be thankful for all God has given you—can also improve mental health and well-being. Singing and giving thanks will naturally lift your spirit and make the wait for what you want or need so much more enjoyable.

56

Give Your Faith in God a Boost

Faith is to believe what you do not see; the reward
of this faith is to see what you believe.

—SAINT AUGUSTINE

Having faith in God isn't always easy, but the reward that Saint Augustine speaks of is real. So are other rewards.

Consider, for instance, this reward: research shows that faith in God mitigates depression. Researchers at McLean Hospital in Belmont, Massachusetts, found that patients who had faith in God had better treatment outcomes. People with strong faith in God were twice as likely to respond to treatment as patients who had little or no faith.

And what does this have to do with contentment?

Regardless of life's circumstances, faith in God has been proven to help people experience better results from medical treatments as well as improved mental health and greater well-being along the way. Over and over, faith in God can be seen to directly improve healing and increase contentment.

When doubt threatens your contentment, think of your faith as a garden and try these three methods to boost your faith:

1. Plant your faith. Read Scripture (this one is a good start), good books, or quotes that are seeds of encouragement and inspiration, reminding you that God is sovereign and He will work out situations for the best (Romans 8:28).

2. Nurture your faith. Put your faith into action. For example, because I have faith that my garden will grow, I plant these seeds and water them regularly. I will watch for weeds of doubt that could choke my plants, and I will pluck them out, being sure to get their roots before they take hold.

3. Harvest your faith. Share your victories—talk about those times when God did strengthen your faith, when you did experience His presence, His peace, His guidance—just as you would share a bountiful harvest of your garden tomatoes. Your messages can inspire, encourage, and remind people that the seemingly impossible is possible.

Before too long, your faith will be flourishing, your contentment will be blossoming, and you will have a bounty to share!

"If I know what
LOVE
is, it is
because of you."

HERMANN HESSE

57

Gather Up the Love

If I know what love is, it is because of you.

—HERMANN HESSE

Regardless of your relationship status, think about the variety of love around you. Here's a list to help:

- Romantic Love is full of passion and desire, but can be short-lived.
- Unconditional Love is selfless, often empowered by God's love, and truly the most radical and transformative.
- Affectionate Love is platonic love between friends and one of the most fulfilling kinds of love we can experience.
- Self-Love is, to be clear, not self*ish*. When we are blessed to be loved in other ways yet still feel discontent, it may be that we forgot to show love and compassion to ourselves.
- Familiar Love is the love between family members and the love between a parent and a child—typically a very strong bond.
- Enduring Love has been nurtured over many years and doesn't require a lot of effort; both partners put in equal efforts.
- Playful Love is often present when you light up the moment this person walks through the door.

In your mind, gather up your loved ones and list their names in a journal. For each, note the kind of love you have for them. You might be delighted to see that your life is full of love to a degree you weren't previously aware of.

To which of these people you listed could you send a love note today?

58

Appreciate the Pure

To the pure, all things are pure!

—MARCEL PROUST

Pure gold. Pure maple syrup. Pure air.

When it serves us, we will always chase what is pure.

When something is labeled as 100 percent pure, we know it's unadulterated and uncontaminated. It's the best, and that's what we want. A certain peace of mind comes with knowing something is 100 percent pure. Unlike things that may be processed and full of preservatives or other unknown ingredients, something pure won't typically harm us. It will likely only heal and nurture us in some way. Sure, some items don't stand up to this criterion, but go along with me for a moment.

When it comes to what we want, we appreciate the pure. We want people's motives and intentions to be pure when they interact with us, don't we? We don't want to discover something in them that was hiding behind a label or not listed among the ingredients. That kind of unsettling discovery can cause a great amount of discontent.

In sharp contrast, think about how sweet something tastes that is 100 percent pure—how robust its flavor is . . . how lovely its scent . . . how brightly it shines. Think, too, about how light you feel when someone with a pure heart comes to you with an unexpected gift. These experiences of purity are blissful moments, but we don't have to wait for external factors to align in order to experience such purity.

Instead, we can ask God's Spirit to remove our own impurities and then cooperate with Him in the process. With His direction, we can go spelunking into the depths of our hearts, mine for the gold, and clear out the dross.

The dross—the impurity—in our lives can take the form of many things, including resentment, anger, bitterness, selfishness, unrighteousness, and so forth. When we cooperate with God's Spirit as He removes the dross, we become purer, and God's pure light can shine through us more brightly. We'll also discover that great contentment and joy dwell in a pure heart, and they're yours to experience with just a little internal housekeeping.

59

Quiet the Inner Critic

The artist doesn't have time to listen to the critics.

—WILLIAM FAULKNER

You don't deserve to be content.

What makes you so special anyway?

Don't get so high-and-mighty; show some humility.

You're good, but not that good.

No one will believe you.

You'll never succeed.

You'll never be truly loved.

Perhaps you've heard these phrases—or variations of these phrases—being whispered somewhere deep in your mind. Or maybe the whisper is not so subtle. In fact, it's more of a shout—perhaps your own voice or maybe someone else's you recall from memory—that can jolt you right out of a cozy, content moment.

What is the one discouraging phrase that you tend to hear repeated over and over and over and over? Pick one. Not sure what to pick? Then go with: *What makes you think you're so special?*

Let this question be the starting point for a conversation between your head and your heart. Your head is the voice of judgment and criticism, both of which are typically rooted somewhere in the past. Those statements are things we've heard other people say, perhaps to us or about us to others, or maybe they are lies we've picked up from the media. The fact is, these thoughts are not your thoughts. They are not original. You did not create them. Yet because they pop up in your mind, you think they're true.

But what does your heart have to say? Ask it. *What makes me so special?* Then listen. What does your heart say to you? Does it remind you how compassionate and giving you are? What a great listener and loyal friend you are? Does your heart call to mind your dreams and passions? Does it replay memories of those times you stayed up all night caring for a loved one or gave a ride to someone in need? Does your heart point you to your ability and intelligence by reminding you of awards you've won? High scores you've achieved? Creativity you've expressed that, as a result, gave others real joy?

These things—all of them . . . and so much more—are some of what make you so special.

It's the curve of your smile, the sound of your laugh, the way you can light up a room when you want to, the way you tear up when you see someone suffering, and even the way you sometimes sing off-key.

You are so uniquely you that you can't be anything but special.

That being the case, the next time you hear your inner critic, thank him for his concern, but let him know you're doing just fine. In fact, you are special just as you are.

And may that truth help you be . . . content.

60

Explore Your Options

Roads . . . don't go anywhere. They stay in
one place, so folks can walk on them.

—L. FRANK BAUM

In the film *The Wizard of Oz*, Dorothy comes to a crossroads. Not knowing
which way to go, she turns to the Scarecrow for answers. He says, "That way
is a very nice way," pointing to the left. "It's pleasant down that way too!"
He points to the right. "Of course, people do go both ways." The Scarecrow
points in both directions.

Sometimes in the midst of a perfectly fine journey, we find ourselves like
Dorothy: we are standing at a crossroads not knowing where to go. Maybe
this counsel will be more helpful than the Scarecrow's.

Consider each option and ask yourself:

- What could I gain from going that way?
- What could I gain from going another way?
- What could I lose?
- What if I just stay here and do nothing?

Now, when you find yourself at a crossroads, it is a time for you to truly
explore your options. In addition to answering the four questions, imagine all
the other options being taken away, leaving you with only one.

Close your eyes. Imagine you've moved forward wholeheartedly with this choice. How do you feel? Are you happy? Sad? What are you thinking? Are you wishing you had chosen that *other* path instead? Ask yourself these questions about each of your possible choices.

Then, for each of the options you're considering, close your eyes and imagine you've chosen something else. How do you feel now that this is your *only* option?

If you notice as you go through these mental exercises that one choice leaves you feeling more content and in alignment with your passions, skills, dreams, goals, and God's plan, perhaps that is the path for you.

61

Remove Temptation

"Everything is permissible" . . . but
not everything is beneficial.

—1 CORINTHIANS 6:12 CSB

We're taught to resist temptation, but how can resisting temptation possibly lead to contentment when the very thing we're tempted by seems the only thing that can bring contentment?

Exercising self-control isn't easy, but it can be the very thing that leads you to the contentment you really want. It takes practice to develop self-control, for sure, and life gives us plenty of opportunities to practice. Doesn't a temptation seem always to be tugging at you, trying to lead you on a path to trouble? Whether you give in is completely up to you.

But take a moment, step back, and stop vilifying those things that are tempting you. Don't condone them! Instead, just remove the label "I can't have this" or "I can't do that." Oftentimes this paradigm shift is the very thing that helps remove the temptation.

After all, we human beings tend to want the very things we're not allowed to have. By first changing the label from "Forbidden" to "Permissible" and then freely choosing what's *truly* beneficial—and therefore what will truly bring ultimate contentment—we can begin to reduce and perhaps even remove temptation from our lives.

So think of the biggest temptations you're facing right now. Then pick one.

What is this temptation in opposition to? For example, if you're tempted by sweets, this might be in opposition to health and wellness. What if you began to think of this temptation as permissible instead of forbidden? Again, you're just having a conversation with yourself. You're not giving in.

Think of that gorgeous homemade cake your coworker brought in when you're on a diet. Think about the slice you so desire as permissible. Of course you're allowed to eat a slice! You're free to choose. I'm not telling you to chow down; I'm simply asking you to imagine that you are *allowed* to. You might also imagine eating it. Imagine, too, what it might taste like.

Next, imagine ten minutes after you've given in to your temptation and eaten that slice, however small it was. What are you feeling after the splurge? Are you content? Or are you now further away from that goal?

Considering the values and goals you're committed to against whatever is tempting you—and then removing the "Forbidden" label—can help to loosen the mental and emotional grip of what otherwise might feel like deprivation. Now you're able to make your choice based on commitment.

This approach to temptation definitely takes practice, but the more you practice and the more often you remove the labels, the more freedom you'll experience.

I AM FOCUSED

I AM STRONG

I CAN DO THIS

62

Master Self-Discipline

Discipline is choosing between what you
want now, and what you want most.

—ABRAHAM LINCOLN

Contentment comes when you overcome temptation and get what you *really* want most. Resisting temptation definitely has its rewards. If you need a little extra help with self-control and discipline, here are five things you can do:

1. Recognize your triggers and avoid them. Think of them like allergies that make you sick, sneezy, achy, and miserable.
2. Know your weaknesses. Can you turn down a different street instead of passing by the bakery on your commute?
3. Ask for help. There are others facing the same temptations you are. Join a group—or start one yourself.
4. Remove temptation. Go back to the exercise on the previous page and explore what it looks like to remove the "forbidden" label.
5. Arm yourself with prayers, quotes, or affirmations. Find one that resonates most. Here are a few to get you started:
   - I can do all things through Christ who strengthens me.
   - My potential to succeed is infinite.
   - I am focused. I am strong. I can do this.

63

Understand Patience

Be patient and tough; someday this
pain will be useful to you.

—OVID

Patience is another character trait that, when added to our lives, brings fulfillment and contentment. It's a word we throw around, often without considering what it means.

Below is a thought-provoking excerpt from "Patience," an essay by nineteenth-century American theologian James W. Alexander.

In its simplest form, patience is a calm and unshaken state of mind, strongly bearing up against a present burden of distress. This may exist without religion. A Stoic or a western savage may endure pain without a murmur. Malefactors have stoutly faced the torments of their penal death. In respect to this, the natural temperament of human beings differs. Some can naturally bear more than others. They have more rigid fibre, or less shrinking nerves, more robust health, or smaller sensibility. The degree of pain is to be measured, not by the force of the blow, but the power of resistance. That which would crush a reed shall leave no mark upon an oak.

When pain comes, however, it is well if we have even natural means of enduring it. But practice, discipline, and exercise add vastly even to this natural fortitude. Fresh soldiers and new recruits quail and fly, but the veteran has looked death in the face. He who has endured once, can endure again. Still more efficacious is the operation of inward principle, adding moral motives to the barely natural power. Education has this for part of its work, to teach the young to bear some burdens, not to fall back at every alarm, nor cry out at every pang. Stern determination will help one to sustain what might at first have seemed intolerable. This is remarkably the case in great and sudden pangs of anguish, for which a resolved mind has prepared itself.

Think about those times when you've cried out with every ounce of energy you had. In what specific ways would stern determination have helped you—and how can stern determination help you now?

And when would having a resolved mind have helped you—and how might a resolved mind be useful in your own life now?

64

Pursue Patience

Patience and Diligence, like faith, remove mountains.

—WILLIAM PENN

Reaching your goals requires patience and persistence; without both, you run the risk of giving up. You see, patience fuels persistence. The more patient you become, the more willing you are to put in the time and effort required to reach your goals. Or, simply put, the more persistent or diligent you will be.

So, take inventory of what makes you impatient. Do you hate being stuck in traffic? Do you want to charge ahead with a project, more interested in the goal than in planning the steps to get there? When working with other people, do you find them moving too slowly and wish you could hurry things along? Impatience comes in many different forms and circumstances.

If you decide you need more patience, here's a challenge that can help you develop that muscle. Choose a project that will require perseverance to complete. Maybe redecorating a room or learning a new skill. Next, promise yourself that you will complete the task without losing your patience. If you feel patience slipping away as you work on the project, stop what you're doing. Take a few deep breaths. Then focus on patience instead of the task. If you need to walk away for a while to relax and calm down, that's fine. Remind yourself that you don't need to finish the project by a certain time. This is an exercise in patience; it's not a race.

Patience is a skill. Keep practicing it one day at a time. After some time and a little work, patience will become a part of your character.

65

Put Patience on Display

Patience is the best remedy for every trouble.

—PLAUTUS

When we put something in a museum, it's on display for everyone who visits. If your patience were featured in the museum of your life, what would people notice?

And this isn't a hypothetical. Your patience—or lack thereof—*is* always on display. Even if you're trying to hide your impatience, it can come out in various forms—your tone of voice, a look, a scowl, a huff, or a general freneticism. Or perhaps you already know that you're not good at hiding your impatience, so you allow yourself to fully act it out. Your impatience quickly turns to anger. Before long, you are speaking angry, hurtful words in a tone that matches. Perhaps you or someone else slams a door. And now both you and the people around you are left feeling disconnected and certainly discontent.

Like many qualities, patience is a muscle to be developed and flexed. Here are a few exercises to help you strengthen this muscle:

1. Take a time-out. Walk away and give yourself—and others—a short break to take a deep breath and reset.
2. Remove the element of surprise. Sometimes impatience happens when something catches us off guard. We had a certain expectation, and our experience is something different. Related to this point, be aware of any persistent triggers, circumstances, or moments in the day when you easily become impatient. For example, if you know

your impatience surges when you come home from work and see your kids' messes, don't let their mess surprise you each time.

3. Practice gratitude. In fact, when you come home from work and before you open the door to your home, come up with three things about your home life that you are grateful for. Be grateful, for instance, that you have a home the kids can make messy, that you have creative, energetic children who aren't sitting in front of a screen, and that you made it home safely.

4. Visualize your ideal response. As you drive home, think about—visualize—your ideal entrance into the house . . . and your ideal reaction to the evidence of your children's play. Before you open the door to your home, visualize yourself speaking joy-filled, love-filled words. Then, when you act according to what you picture, savor the contentment that comes when you are that person.

5. Laugh. Begin to look for the absolute absurdity in life's everyday situations. Think about the fact that every single day you come home to kid toys everywhere. Really? They can't have the mess picked up *even once?* It's crazy!

Work on these five exercises, and it won't be long before your patience can be proudly displayed full-time in the museum of your life.

"WHATEVER YOU ARE, BE A GOOD ONE"

WILLIAM
MAKEPEACE THACKERAY

66

Do Excellent Work

Whatever you are, be a good one.

—WILLIAM MAKEPEACE THACKERAY

If you aren't content at work, ask yourself, "What can I do to bring excellence to my assignments and responsibilities?"

Something very interesting happens when we intentionally strive for a certain level of excellence in the work we do. A job we may have dreaded becomes a new challenge. A task we avoided becomes more like a game. *What can I do to bring my best to my work?* becomes a goal, a purpose statement. You'll find yourself looking for new opportunities to excel.

If you think this approach doesn't apply to you, that your job is somehow different, I assure you that you're mistaken. Whether you're the CEO or a janitor, an artist or a store clerk, you can do that work with excellence. And this principle doesn't apply only to work that generates a paycheck.

Think for a moment about what you want from work—besides the obvious paycheck. How do you want to feel about your work? Maybe like it matters? Like you're the best at what you do? What are you really passionate about? What kind of work makes you excited and happy? How can you bring those elements into your work and tasks?

In Paul's letter to the Colossians, he said, "Whatever you do, work at it with all your heart, as working for the Lord, not for human masters, since you know that you will receive an inheritance from the Lord as a reward. It is the Lord Christ you are serving" (3:23–24). There's God's call to excellence. And, yes, "whatever you do" includes filing papers or sweeping the floor.

67

Express Lovingkindness

Even a little gift may be vast with loving kindness.

—THEOCRITUS

Through the apostle Paul, God commands us to "clothe [ourselves] with compassion, kindness, humility, gentleness and patience. . . . And over all these virtues put on love" (Colossians 3:12, 14).

In Matthew 7:12, Jesus put it this way: "Do to others what you would have them do to you." By working hard to follow that one rule, you can significantly increase your ability to be kind and loving to anyone.

And loving others isn't always easy. Consider the loving act of forgiveness—and some of the horrendous acts of betrayal and cruelty that people have forgiven. Such forgiveness is only possible when people set aside what they want and choose to love others with the love of God.

In addition to the act of forgiveness, another act of lovingkindness that demonstrates God's love is accepting people who have different opinions. Realizing that God gives everyone freedom to have their own ideas can help you bring lovingkindness to situations that otherwise might provoke anger or resentment. You can also learn to disagree without criticism or judgment. When what you want doesn't align with what others want, make peace your priority. Try not to argue, and if you must disagree, then do so with respect.

A third way to show lovingkindness is by tolerating the things people do that irritate you. Maybe your husband tells the same joke over and over, your friend has a tendency to be late, or your kids put empty milk cartons in the refrigerator. Don't let little things become big things. If you have to reprimand, do so gently. And why not laugh at the joke for the hundredth time? Your husband is just trying to bring a little fun into the world.

Ask God to change your perspective in ways that will help boost your lovingkindness. As you grow in His love, you might also discover that your level of contentment grows too.

"A kindness is never wasted."

68

Grow Your Kindness

A kindness is never wasted.

—AESOP

God can take even our smallest acts of kindness and increase their impact exponentially. You may never know how far your kindness has reached. May this poem by Edgar A. Guest inspire you today to see what others want and need.

KINDNESS

One never knows
How far a word of kindness goes;
One never sees
How far a smile of friendship flees.
Down, through the years,
The deed forgotten reappears.
One kindly word
The souls of many here has stirred.
Man goes his way
And tells with every passing day,
Until life's end:
"Once unto me he played the friend."
We cannot say
What lips are praising us today. . . .
But kindness lives
Beyond the memory of him who gives.

69

Embrace Change

The definition of insanity is doing the same thing over
and over again, but expecting different results.

—ALBERT EINSTEIN

The mere idea of change can sometimes disquiet the soul, and an actual but unexpected change can rock your world. You're going along, everything seems to be working just fine, and it's smooth sailing. Then seemingly out of nowhere—*bam!* Something changes.

Change, however, doesn't have to cause unrest or panic. Not convinced? Think of a work of art. It begins with a blank canvas and evolves. Changes happen along the way. An artist might begin with an idea of what she wants the finished piece to look like, yet end up with something different. Something that nevertheless satisfies and pleases.

Contentment develops in a similar way. You can imagine it however you choose and attempt to make it whatever you want. The only requirement along the way is the *willingness* to change or accept change. I'll explain.

Consider these questions to determine where you are on the path to contentment:

- Do you have a better idea of what true contentment is?
- In what aspects of your life do you find the most contentment?
- Do you have a clear idea of where you are on your path to true contentment?

- Do you have a clear idea of where you'd like to be?
- What changes do you want to make to get closer to your idea of contentment?

The bottom line is this: if you want a different result—if you want the kind of contentment you have yet to experience—you'll have to do something different than you've been doing. This "something different" will mean some degree of change in your attitude, actions, or perspective. If you're willing to make some changes to all three, get ready for a tidal wave of contentment!

70

Broadcast Your Blessings

Talk about your blessings more than
you talk about your burdens.

—UNKNOWN

Let's talk about difficult times for a moment. Living with contentment does not mean you won't face challenges. It doesn't mean you won't struggle. It doesn't mean you're immune to loss or natural disasters or health issues or scary medical diagnoses or global pandemics.

However, as you begin to live a life of contentment, you will be well equipped to handle trials with more grace and ease. And if you're just now exploring what it means to be content in the midst of a storm, at first it may seem unnatural not to talk about your burdens. After all, isn't that what most people do? Maybe, but I'm suggesting something different.

However, I'm *not* suggesting that you ignore the pain or completely avoid sharing what is going on. I'm simply saying, let your words about your blessings be louder. Instead of broadcasting your burdens on loudspeaker, blast your blessings to the world.

If you're ready to think more deeply about those burdens, consider the blessings *resulting from* the challenge you're facing. Are you learning to be more compassionate? To extend grace more freely? Have you connected with people you wouldn't have otherwise? Or stopped taking someone for granted? Have you learned how to ask for help—and let someone else help you, giving them the opportunity to be great? Or how did *you* get to be great in this situation?

I encourage you to look for the blessings among or within the burdens. The blessings are there. This doesn't discount your feelings or anything you're going through. If you let them, awareness of the blessings will provide a softer refuge for your burdened heart.

71

Sharpen Your Observation Skills

Observation, not old age, brings wisdom.

—PUBLILIUS SYRUS

Sister Wendy Beckett was a Catholic nun and British art historian whose documentaries on art history were popular in the 1990s. Sister Wendy often spoke about the art of observation as it relates to painting. She once shared this recurring experience: "Again and again I've taken quick glances and then, for some reason, I've got to sit before a picture waiting, and it's opened up like one of those Japanese flowers that you put into water, and something I thought wasn't worth more than a casual, respectful glance begins to open up depth after depth of meaning."

Think about Sister Wendy's words. When have you given something a quick glance and then thought about that moment later? Or when have you been compelled to look more closely at something?

Each day, God puts His works of art all around you. If something catches your eye today, don't hurry past it, or you could miss something wonderful—and miss out on a moment of worship and contentment.

Stop. Wait. Look more closely at God's amazing creation.

72

Come to Your Senses

I who am blind can give one hint to those who see: Use your
eyes as if tomorrow you would be stricken blind. And the same
method can be applied to the other senses. Hear the music of
voices, the song of a bird, the mighty strains of an orchestra, as
if you would be stricken deaf tomorrow. Touch each object as
if tomorrow your tactile sense would fail. Smell the perfume of
flowers, taste with relish each morsel, as if tomorrow you could
never smell and taste again. Make the most of every sense; glory in
the beauty which the world in all the facets of pleasure reveals to
you through the several means of contact which Nature provides.
But of all the senses, I am sure that sight is the most delightful.

—HELEN KELLER

What lovely words of wisdom! And what a powerful call to use your mind and
memory to store everyday sensory experiences that one day you may not
be able to experience at all.

You've likely collected all sorts of thoughts, some of which were gath-
ered by your senses. Many of these thoughts are lovely and remarkable, and
these could—when brought to the forefront of your mind and dusted off—
bring you contentment, comfort, and joy.

Find a quiet place to think. Then jot down your answers to these five
questions about your life up to this point:

- What is the most beautiful sight you've seen?
- The loveliest sound you've heard?

- The most delicious food you've tasted?
- The most extraordinary thing you've touched?
- The most pleasing scent you've smelled?

Don't stop with those few thoughts you've just unearthed from the past. Pull out even more. Savor those rich reminders of all the good and wonderful experiences God has blessed you with.

73

Celebrate!

We think there is endless time to live but we
never know which moment is last. So share, care,
love, and celebrate every moment of life.

—UNKNOWN

It's easy to celebrate certain occasions: weddings, birthdays, anniversaries, new babies, and holidays.

But don't miss the opportunity to celebrate other times and events, both everyday and remarkable. Have fun creating your own special occasions. Need some ideas? Okay!

Who in your life could use some celebrating? What little victories might be the focal point? What silly "National Something Day" can prompt some family fun? And here are some additional reasons to celebrate the people around you:

- A good test score
- A raise or promotion
- A new job
- A new home
- Reaching your goal weight
- Hitting a fitness milestone
- A new relationship
- A long-standing relationship
- A new friendship

You can create all kinds of opportunities to celebrate and honor the people in your life. And don't forget to celebrate *you* from time to time. Treat yourself to something you enjoy. Take the day off, read a book, watch a movie, go to the spa, walk with a friend, bake a cake—whatever your heart can dream up!

Be sure to celebrate often!

74

Offer Praise!

The praise of the praiseworthy is above all rewards.

—J. R. R. TOLKIEN

Everyone benefits from praise. Having someone compliment your commendable deeds and accomplishments can give a big boost to your contentment. Praise, however, goes beyond a compliment. It provides the recipient a deeper sense of being valued. Think about times when praise made you feel more content. Did praise come in the form of words, a warm hug, or an unexpected celebration? We have many different ways of offering praise for a job well done.

Today, shift your thoughts from yourself to others. Make it your mission to recognize and praise people and their commendable acts. Offer praise to family members, friends, coworkers, and even strangers:

- To the child who sits quietly through a long school day: "You behaved so well in school today. Good job!"
- To the IT person who solved your computer problem: "You know so much about solving these issues. I don't know what I'd have done without you!"
- To the crossing guard at your child's school: "Thanks so much for keeping my child safe. I appreciate you!"

Be generous with your praise. And focus on praising those small acts that might otherwise go unnoticed.

75

Sing Out Loud!

Life is better when you sing.

—UNKNOWN

Do you know what happens inside your body when you sing? Your body releases chemicals called endorphins that reduce stress, relieve pain, and trigger positive feelings. When you sing, you also breathe more deeply and inhale more oxygen. As you sing, you exercise your diaphragm, which stimulates your very important vagus nerve. This nerve—that runs from your neck to your abdomen—turns off the "fight or flight" reflex, which activates your relaxation response.

Singing, in general, will have these effects on us. And when we combine singing with lyrics that inspire us, we amplify the good feelings that music brings.

So let's think about singing. First, what is *your* song? What's that song that, when it comes on, you know all the words and you can't help but sing along? Do you sing at the top of your lungs? Good! This means you're really getting the benefits!

- What's your favorite love song?
- Your favorite happy song?
- Your favorite silly song?
- Your favorite song to sing and dance to?

Turn it on, play it loud, and sing it proud! Life is better when you sing!

76
Determine What Is True

In the popular television game show *To Tell the Truth* (1956–1968), celebrity panelists tried to decide which of three contestants was telling the truth about his or her occupation. While all in good fun, the show revealed just how easy it is to be deceived. Lies are everywhere. Scams are everywhere. The Federal Trade Commission warns of scams involving imposters, debt collection, identity theft, and more. Romance scams, especially those where couples meet online, are number one.

Simply put, scammers steal contentment as they steal other things. Jesus warned about them. He said, "Be careful of false prophets. They come to you looking gentle like sheep, but they are really dangerous like wolves" (Matthew 7:15 NCV).

To combat this, in Philippians 4:8, when Paul gave advice about where to center our thoughts, he reminded us, "Think about the things that are true" (NCV). He wrote in 1 Thessalonians 5:21, "Test everything. Keep what is good" (NCV).

If you find yourself questioning whether something is the truth or a lie, here is a plan you can put into action:

- Don't be in a hurry to accept something as truth.
- Do your own research. Gather the facts yourself rather than relying on what someone tells you.

- If you have even a bit of uncertainty, dig deeper.
- Talk to other people; get their perspective and advice.
- Ask God to give you wisdom and the ability to discern truth from lies.

As you practice testing the truth, you will be less likely to be deceived.

77

Silence the Stress

Who begins too much accomplishes little.

—GERMAN PROVERB

The stress that comes when we feel overwhelmed robs us of contentment. When thoughts of everything we have to do pile up, we might panic. Sometimes we can't figure out where to begin or how to get it all done!

Stress comes when we're trying to hold all of life's details in place so that we don't drop the ball. We're afraid we'll forget something important, and we worry there's not adequate time to actually do all of the things we think we need to do. This convergence of fear, worry, and stress can paralyze us, leaving us confused and unable to accomplish very much—and then we have to clean up the messes caused by the things we didn't do.

I encourage you to research the incredible productivity experts out there, who offer wonderful methodologies for avoiding the stress that comes with being overwhelmed. In the meantime, try this basic exercise:

1. Make as thorough a to-do list as you can. Include all the deadlines and appointments you're currently aware of.
2. Close your eyes. Take a moment to breathe—and to see whether you're forgetting anything.
3. Put the appointments, deadlines, and tasks on your calendar.
4. Is there a conflict somewhere? Are you double-booked? Is there a day that simply does not work? That's okay; it happens to everyone. Communicate with the people involved and see what you can work

out. If no solution is agreed to, simply let the people impacted know that you won't be able to do what you said you would do. And if you feel so inclined, ask how that fact impacts them and what, if anything, you can do to make it up to them or to clean up the mess.

5. Returning to your to-do list, determine what things you can set aside for a later time. Which of the items are simply a nice idea, and which are must-dos? Be honest with yourself and give yourself permission to let go of those things that you truly don't need to deal with right now. As for those items that stay on the list, schedule them—put them on the calendar—so that you will have ample time to get them done.

Now take a look at your calendar. What's on the agenda for today? Tackle the first task. Simply getting this one thing done should greatly reduce your sense of being overwhelmed and the stress it causes. Enjoy even the hint of contentment that results!

"Our life
is what
our thoughts
make it."

MARCUS AURELIUS

78

Filter Your Thoughts

Our life is what our thoughts make it.

—MARCUS AURELIUS

Does a cup of aromatic coffee or tea add to your feelings of contentment? It does for me. What is your preferred method of brewing? Tea requires a tea bag or strainer, and coffee needs a filter. Without one, you would have a cup filled with tea leaves or bitter coffee grounds.

When it comes to brewing coffee, we can choose paper filters, metal filters, basket filters, and filters built into pots to separate the solids from the liquid. If you think about the many ways of brewing coffee for the best flavor—pour over, French press, moka pot, syphon—your thoughts can start swimming in coffee!

Have you considered that our thoughts need a filter too? After all, what we think about has a lot to do with how we feel and behave. Thoughts shape us. Good thoughts build contentment, and disturbing thoughts tear it down. Some thoughts stick. They can trap us and refuse to let go.

Try this today. Be more aware of your thoughts. Filter them as they come. Catch those that are unpleasant and throw them out. Allow the good thoughts to linger and bring you contentment. Pay close attention to thoughts that seem to get stuck. Decide whether they are worth hanging on to or need to be filtered out.

Your thoughts will never be 100 percent pure. You're human, and nobody is perfect! But as you practice being aware of your thoughts, you will become more skilled at filtering the good ones from the bad.

79

Create Some Beautiful Memories

It is better to create than to learn!
Creating is the essence of life.

—JULIUS CAESAR

Think of life being like an art gallery. Certain images catch your eye and cause you to stop. Some images are so beautiful they travel directly from your eyes to your heart. You not only savor them in the moment, but you also hold them tight in your memory so you can retrieve them later and enjoy them again. Beautiful memories can become treasures and heirlooms. Imagine your children telling their children about things you did with them when they were young.

We can create beautiful memories with our children in many ways. Here are just a few:

- Introduce your children to the world of your childhood. Take them to places you loved to go. Show them things you most enjoyed doing. Weave your story into each activity so your children can see the past through your eyes.
- Make the most of the present. Set your thoughts on the gift of time and making new memories. After doing something together, ask questions: What made this activity special? What do you think you'll remember most? Do you think that someday you'll tell your kids about what we did together?

- Finally, record your memories as photos, videos, and even stories you write down. Perhaps make scrapbooks, photo albums, or gift books to give to your children when they become adults.

Bask in the beauty of your memories. Let them fill your heart and enjoy the warmth and contentment they bring.

80

Savor Each Season

I wonder if the snow *loves* the trees and fields, that
it kisses them so gently? And then it covers them up
snug, you know, with a white quilt; and perhaps it says,
"Go to sleep, darlings, till the summer comes again."

—LEWIS CARROLL

What is more beautiful than the changing seasons? In his book *Adventures in Contentment*, Ray Stannard Baker shared these words of agreement:

In all the days of my life I have never been so well content as I am this spring. Last summer I thought I was happy, the fall gave me a finality of satisfaction, the winter imparted perspective, but spring conveys a wholly new sense of life.

Like the earth itself, our lives have seasons. Let's learn to better appreciate them.

Think about how with each season in nature you've grown and become even better.

Think, too, about any occurrences of—figuratively speaking—fall, winter, spring, and summer in your life.

And consider some ways life is like a perpetual spring, offering newness, vitality, and hope.

81

Enjoy a Poem for all Seasons

Each moment of the year has its own beauty.

—RALPH WALDO EMERSON

Also celebrating the beauty of each season is this poem by Alan L. Strang. Take your time reading the words, imagining each season as it's described.

THE SEASONS

SPRING

Spring time is here with its sunshine and showers,
All nature is waking from its long winter sleep.
The gardens are blooming with beautiful flowers,
The song-birds are carolling melodies sweet.

SUMMER

The summer comes with glaring heat,
And we will have vacation;
We pack our grips for the seashore trips,
Or other recreation.

AUTUMN

The harvest moon is shining bright,
The leaves are falling everywhere;
How glorious is the autumn night,
How cool and bracing is the air.

WINTER

Jack frost is stalking through the land,
The ground is covered white, with snow.
We like to sit beside the fire
And tell the tales of long ago.

82

Gear Up for Great Beginnings

And so with the sunshine and the great bursts of
leaves growing on the trees, just as things grow in
fast movies, I had that familiar conviction that life
was beginning over again with the summer.

—F. SCOTT FITZGERALD

If you're in a bleak season of life right now, remember that winter doesn't last forever. Spring is coming, bringing a new beginning and brand-new energy.

Winter—metaphorically as well as physically—can be difficult because of the absence of light and warmth. Winter is also a time of quiet, of slowing down. The world is absent of leaves and flowers and most animals. There are fewer signs of life all around us.

But I assure you, the blessings of life are present and plentiful. We tend to look at circumstances through the lens of our preferences. We *prefer* sunshine. We *prefer* longer days. We *prefer* seventy-degree weather.

Perhaps the winter you are going through has become a time of survival mode. What have you learned so far that can help bring light to the winter darkness? What might warm your heart? What could God be teaching you this season? What might this season be preparing you for?

Just as winter is necessary in the life cycle of our world, what you are going through is happening for a reason even though you can't even begin to comprehend right now what that reason might be. And just as spring is a time for renewal, what sort of renewal might God have in store for you as your winter passes? Let His sovereignty over your circumstances—over your winter and your survival mode—infuse your heart and soul with peace and even contentment despite trying times.

> The year's at the spring
> And day's at the morn;
> Morning's at seven;
> The hillside's dew-pearled;
> The lark's on the wing;
> The snail's on the thorn;
> God's in His heaven-
> All's right with the world!

—Robert Browning, from "Pippa Passes" (1841)

83

Add a Little Beauty

A man should hear a little music, read a little poetry,
and see a fine picture every day of his life, in order
that worldly cares may not obliterate the sense of the
beautiful which God has implanted in the human soul.

—JOHANN WOLFGANG VON GOETHE

Can you imagine living with every day full of music, poetry, and beautiful artwork? You don't have to work for a symphony or a museum to experience this. It's not hard to let a song or a poem accompany you throughout the day, and we have many opportunities to add "a fine picture" to our everyday life. Not only can we hang things on our walls or put them on refrigerators, but even little electronic canvases like smartphone backgrounds, laptop backgrounds, and social media profiles can be places to add elements of beauty and contentment to our days.

Speaking of social media, consider sharing little treasures of music, poetry, and artwork in your newsfeed so that others in your life could experience and those so that—as Goethe noted above—"Worldly cares may not obliterate the sense of the beautiful which God has implanted in the human soul."

Read those words again: "the sense of the beautiful which God has implanted in the human soul." The ability to recognize the beautiful is innately part of us. We are drawn to beauty: to view it, to experience it, to create it, and to share it.

What beauty will you share today?

84

Know That Joy Is Coming

I consider that our present sufferings are not worth
comparing with the glory that will be revealed in us.

—ROMANS 8:18

When we're going through hard times, it's not easy to set our thoughts on what is good. Lisa Beamer knew that. When her husband, Todd, was killed on 9/11, Lisa had to re-create life without him. To get through the darkest days, she turned to God.

A passenger aboard United Airlines Flight 93, Todd Beamer is a national hero. He organized a group of passengers to take down the hijackers before it could crash into its target: the White House. After reciting the Lord's Prayer and the Twenty-third Psalm, Todd spoke these famous last words: "Are you ready? Okay. Let's roll."

In the aftermath of her husband's death, Lisa thought about heaven and God's gift of eternal life. She trusted that one day she would be there with Him and with Todd. She contemplated ways God had prepared her for life after Todd's death, and she focused on the fact that God was providing for her needs. Lisa recognized God's love for her through the acts of others and through comforting scriptures. Gradually, Lisa worked through her grief, helped by a tight hold on her faith and her choice to keep her thoughts centered on God. She went on to coauthor *Let's Roll: Ordinary People, Extraordinary Courage* to help others dealing with grief. Life wasn't the same for Lisa, but life still had blessings in store for her.

And blessings are also in store for you.

Take a moment to look back on some of your rough seasons. What joys followed despite the perhaps indescribable pain of those times?

If you're in a rough spot now, hold tight, dear reader. Joy is coming!

85

Be Happy with What You Have

Be happy with what you have and are, be generous
with both, and you won't have to hunt for happiness.

—WILLIAM E. GLADSTONE

Aesop tells this little story of the crab and the fox:

> One day a crab grew disgusted with the sands in which he lived. He decided to take a stroll to the meadow not far inland. There he would find better fare than briny water and sand mites. So off he crawled to the meadow. But there a hungry Fox spied him, and in a twinkling, ate him up, both shell and claw.

A small story with a big message: *Be content with your lot.*

True contentment doesn't mean you never move forward or take risks. But there is a significant difference between moving forward and acting foolishly out of disgust—like the crab in Aesop's story. Instead, with each passing moment, prayerfully make wise decisions and then trust God that, whatever happens, you'll be okay.

True contentment means choosing to be okay with your lot in the moment while at the same time preparing to move forward—with appreciation.

86

Identify Your Role Models

The legacy of heroes is the memory of a great
name and the inheritance of a great example.

—BENJAMIN DISRAELI

We can learn more about being content by studying people who have mastered it. Just as budding artists study the works of great masters, you and I can study those who have learned and mastered the art of contentment.

Identify those people in your world who seem settled and content in their lives:

- Notice how they act and react to whatever comes their way.
- What evidence do you see that their behavior is rooted in love, joy, peace, patience, kindness, goodness, faithfulness, gentleness, and self-control because of the fruit of God's presence within them?
- Focus on specific behaviors you would like to incorporate in your own life to improve your level of contentment.
- Experiment! Add some of those behaviors to your daily routine and see what happens.

In addition to observing the people in your life who live with contentment, seek wisdom from those individuals you know who:

- Hold the same values and share the same Christian faith as you
- Have a clear idea of what they want in life

- Have worked through difficult times and emerged content
- Willingly forgive
- Are patient
- Exercise self-control

Ask these people questions. Find out what they've learned about contentment.

The Greek philosopher Epictetus said, "One of the best ways to elevate your character is to emulate worthy role models." Some of the best life lessons you ever learn might come from those people whose behavior you admire. It is within your power to find true contentment, and surrounding yourself with positive role models, learning from them, and assimilating those lessons into your life will help you do just that.

87

Let Adversity Be a Teacher

Although the world is full of suffering, it
is also full of the overcoming of it.

—HELEN KELLER

Nobody wants trouble. That anything bad could happen is a thought we shove to the backs of our minds, and even the idea of trouble can give us chills. Yet everyone experiences tough times to one degree or another.

And throughout history, people have overcome adversity by holding tight to their God. In the Bible, we see Daniel, Joseph, Job, Paul, Jesus, and many others trust God to be with them. More contemporary stories of triumph over adversity include Helen Keller, who was deaf and blind since infancy; Darlene Deibler Rose, a missionary during World War II who developed beriberi when she was sent to prison camp; Nick Vujicic, an inspirational Christian speaker and author who was born without limbs; Elisabeth Elliot, whose missionary husband was killed by the Auca tribe in eastern Ecuador and who later returned to those people as a missionary herself; Corrie ten Boom, who helped many Jews escape the Nazi Holocaust during World War II; and Holocaust survivor Viktor Frankl, whose book *Man's Search for Meaning* has inspired the world.

If you hear Corrie ten Boom's story, you'll learn that when the Nazis found out she and her family were helping Jews escape persecution, the Nazis arrested the ten Booms and put them in concentration camps. The conditions were beyond terrible there, but Corrie kept her focus on God and on helping others. She held secret prayer meetings and taught the Bible. After the war ended and she was free, Corrie ten Boom continued to serve God by sharing her story around the world. By God's grace, she was even able to forgive the prison guards who had treated her so badly.

Corrie and many others have faced adversity, but putting their faith in their faithful God, they knew that whatever happened, they would be okay. Seeing how ordinary people have faced adversity with extraordinary faith in God can help you prepare for difficult times, and their stories of triumph will inspire you.

"I trust,
and nothing
that happens
disturbs
my trust."

HELEN KELLER

88

Opt for Optimism

> Optimism is the faith that leads to achievement.
> Nothing can be done without hope and confidence.
>
> —HELEN KELLER

The amazing Helen Keller—an accomplished woman who was blind, deaf, and, as a result, mute for years—is one of the greatest teachers of contentment, optimism, and gratitude. Below is an excerpt from her essay "Optimism."

Most people measure their happiness in terms of physical pleasure and material possession. Could they win some visible goal which they have set on the horizon, how happy they would be! Lacking this gift or that circumstance, they would be miserable. If happiness is to be so measured, I who cannot hear or see have every reason to sit in a corner with folded hands and weep. If I am happy in spite of my deprivations, if my happiness is so deep that it is a faith, so thoughtful that it becomes a philosophy of life—if, in short, I am an optimist, my testimony to the creed of optimism is worth hearing. As sinners stand up in meeting and testify to the goodness of God, so one who is called afflicted may rise up in gladness of conviction and testify to the goodness of life. . . .

I trust, and nothing that happens disturbs my trust. I recognize the beneficence of the power which we all worship as supreme—Order, Fate, the Great Spirit, Nature, God. I recognize this power in the sun that makes all things grow and keeps life afoot.

89

Look Beyond Your Circumstances

Circumstances don't make the man,
they only reveal him to himself.

—EPICTETUS

Chances are, you're not facing the kind of extreme circumstances that Helen Keller or Viktor Frankl did. That statement is not intended to downplay your circumstances or diminish your pain. The intention is to offer some perspective and, as a result, some encouragement. Learning to shift our perspective and seeing beyond our current circumstances is a process, and the more we practice, the more proficient we become.

Now, you might have noticed that, in this book, we circle back and revisit certain themes. As you practiced some of the exercises, new paradigms and new perspectives began to emerge. You may be in the same circumstances you were in when you began this journey toward contentment. But now you may be able to see beyond your current circumstances. The walls of your prison of suffering may have begun crumbling.

It's absolutely okay if you haven't reached that point of being content in all circumstances. That kind of learning and growing can be a lifelong process for all of us, and it's something you'll get better at over time.

The imprisoned apostle Paul—possibly the world's first remote teacher—wrote letters to instruct and encourage early believers. In chapter 12 of his letter to the Romans, for instance, Paul reminded these Christians to use the gifts and talents that God blessed them with in service to Him and His people (Romans 12:3–8). Paul directed the Roman believers to "think about the things that are good and worthy of praise. Think about the things that are true and honorable and right and pure and beautiful and respected" (Philippians 4:8 NCV). Both putting our love into action and thinking on good things can fuel and ignite our contentment.

Paul also made this amazing statement: "I have learned to be content whatever the circumstances" (Philippians 4:11). He had come to understand that contentment had nothing to do with the present situation. After all, in the bleak environment of a cold prison cell, Paul continued to focus on God and serve Him by teaching others about Jesus. For Paul, contentment meant trusting in God, obeying His commands, and being strengthened by His grace.

90

Keep Love and Contentment Near

Do you want to know how Contentment looks? Some
people think she is the most beautiful among all the fairies.

—CAROLINE SNOWDEN GUILD

Let us for a moment enter into a children's fantasy tale where lighthearted
wisdom abounds. The following is an excerpt from *Violet: A Fairy Story* by
nineteenth-century writer Caroline Snowden Guild:

> So it would be if every little girl and boy kept two good fairies, like Love
> and Contentment, flying about with them.
>
> How the grass glittered with dew! how the slender wild flowers
> were bowed down with its weight!—pearl and diamond beads strung all
> along the stems, and edging every petal. Children who keep in bed until
> eight o'clock know very little about the beauty of summer mornings.
> Perhaps, even if they did arise in time, they would be afraid of wetting
> their shoes in the grass; but Violet was very poor, you know, and never
> wore a shoe in her life, and lived out of doors so much that she was not
> in the least delicate.
>
> As soon as the sunshine had crept near their nests among the green
> boughs of the wood, all the wild birds began to flutter about and sing such
> loud, clear, sweet songs that Violet could not help joining the chorus;
> and anyone else would have known that fairies Love and Contentment

were singing loudest of all. Violet heard their music, but supposed it came from the birds. How she wanted to fly away with them, up among the beautiful rosy clouds! but Love whispered in her ear—

"Won't your mother want you, little girl, at home? Cannot you help her there?" and just then a bird fluttered away from a dew-wet bough, dashing a whole shower of drops in Violet's face. Instead of being angry, she laughed, and shouted—

"Do it again, bird. If I can't fly away with you, you may wash my face before you go. Do it again."

But the bird was soon out of sight among the clouds, and Violet, with these pearly dewdrops clustering in her golden hair, went dancing down the hill.

So it would be, that you would keep the two good fairies, Love and Contentment, flying about you.

91

Read a Good Book

Reading books can change your life. Books open up new worlds, introduce new ideas, and offer new perspectives. If something isn't working well in your life, perhaps a book can help shed some new light on a subject or help you see a situation differently. Books can help you get unstuck.

As our little book nears its end, consider the following:

- What is your favorite book?
- Who is your favorite author?
- What's the last book you read that really made a difference in your life?
- Which book has had the greatest impact on you?
- If you read fiction, which characters do you admire—and why?

Books are a lovely and generous gift from writer to reader. Someone with a message to share sat down, opened their mind and heart, and penned words in the hope of touching other souls with their story, their learnings, their observations, and their imagination. This invisible yet intimate connection between writer and reader is powerful. After all, a book can transport a suffering reader to an experience of full-fledged joy.

It is said, "When the student is ready, the teacher appears," and I would suggest that when the reader is ready, the book appears.

Which book is calling out to you?

Which books have been sitting on your bookshelves just begging to be read?

What books have been gifted to you by a friend or a loved one who wants to share something with you?

You just might be surprised by the timely messages you find, the new tools you discover, and the uplifting perspectives just waiting for you.

92

Submit to What You Don't Like

The amiable Jemima was always contented and good-humored, even when she was not in a state agreeable to her wishes; and, by learning to submit to what she did not like, when it could not be altered, she obtained the love of everybody who knew her, and passed through life with less trouble than people usually experience; for, by making it a rule to comply with her situation, she always enjoyed the comforts it afforded, and suffered as little as possible from its inconvenience.

—MARY ANN KILNER

Below is a delightful excerpt from *Jemima Placid; or the Advantage of Good-Nature* by Mary Ann Kilner, a prolific writer of children's books during the late eighteenth century.

Say, why should I fretful my fate so lament,
Since pleasure still waits on the smile of content?
Will the clouds soon disperse, if indignant I frown?
And the rain cease in torrents the village to drown?
Will the thunder's loud peal be then hush'd into peace?
And the storm, at my bidding, its violence cease?

Will the sun for my anger discover its ray,
And at once all the beauties of nature display?
Then Ellen, pray tell me, what joy should I find,
In the discord of passion, the storm of the mind?
Though the elements will not resign to my sway,
My temper, I trust, reason's voice shall obey;
Let me make to my fate my desires resign,
And the joys of contentment will ever be mine.

93

Choose Wise Words to Live By

Once you learn to read, you will be forever free.

—FREDERICK DOUGLASS

Warning: The following books will move you. They will stir your soul, make you laugh, make you cry, inspire you, challenge you, and offer you wisdom. Not all are lighthearted; some are extraordinary accounts of triumph over unimaginable adversity. These books are powerful; these books will change you.

When you're ready, explore these great books that—among others—have impacted the world:

- *The Diary of a Young Girl* by Anne Frank
- *The Diving Bell and the Butterfly* by Jean-Dominique Bauby
- *I Am Malala* by Malala Yousafzai
- *I Know Why the Caged Bird Sings* by Maya Angelou
- *Jonathan Livingston Seagull* by Richard Bach
- *The Little Prince* by Antoine de Saint-Exupéry
- *Man's Search for Meaning* by Viktor Frankl
- *Night* by Elie Wiesel
- *The Story of My Life* by Helen Keller

Don't hesitate to add other titles to this list. And imagine the impact if, for a season, you read only inspirational books like these.

94

Learn to Receive

The greatest gift is a portion of thyself.

—RALPH WALDO EMERSON

"It's better to give than to receive."

How often we heard that growing up—usually when we weren't willing to part with something beloved or we simply didn't want to share. Yet this idea may be ingrained at a young age, blossoming when we are older into a struggle to receive. We find ourselves resisting when someone tries to do anything nice for us. Not until I was an adult did I realize that in order for someone to give, there has to be someone to receive. That someone will be you sometimes, and sometimes it will be me.

Whether you give or receive, you and the other person will both be blessed. When someone has an opportunity to be the giver and chooses you to receive, you are blessed by what the giver was blessed to give.

When you receive, you give someone the blessing of giving. Consider these everyday situations as opportunities for such a double blessing:

- Allow someone to open a door for you.
- Let someone pick up the check at lunch.
- Accept someone's offer to make a meal for you.
- Let someone drive you to an event.
- Welcome a coworker's help with a project.

How many times have you resisted offerings like these? Consider how many times you have pushed back with "No. Thank you, but you don't have to do that."

Think.

Each opportunity listed—and countless others—is a way to accept love from the giver. Whenever someone offers you something, focus on and affirm their generous spirit. Also, be mindful that they're trying to communicate their love for you. They want you to know they love you, they are here for you, they appreciate you, and they just want to do something nice for you.

Are you willing to receive as well as give?

95

Look for Everyday Miracles

Miracles, in the sense of phenomena we
cannot explain, surround us on every hand:
life itself is the miracle of miracles.

—BERNARD SHAW

When you hear the word *miracle*, what comes to mind?

Maybe you think of something big like an otherworldly healing or an odds-defying rescue. Such big miracles do happen, but smaller miracles surround us every day. Too many of them we take for granted. Consider, for instance, that life itself is a miracle. Every breath is a gift from God. Every sunrise and sunset is evidence of the miraculous rhythm God built into the universe that He created and holds together.

The connection between our mind and our body is a miracle, and so is the body's unique ability to heal itself. Gravity holds us down so we don't fly up into the ether. Plants grow and life flows and seasons change. Birds and butterflies and whales somehow know the path from home to their breeding grounds and back again. Bats map their surroundings through sound. Fireflies light up to attract their mates, pets sense our emotions and react accordingly—and this list of life's little, everyday miracles is endless.

What about the miracle of *you*?

What about the everyday miracles in your own life that you might have begun to take for granted?

Take time today to make a step toward the miraculous.

Think about daily miracles, those logic-defying things you take for granted. List at least three for each of these categories:

- At home
- At work
- In nature
- In relationships
- Inside your body

When you learn to recognize miracles, you become more aware of God's perfectly designed universe. Miracles challenge logic as they glorify God.

96

Shelter in Peace

There is nothing like staying at home for real comfort.

—JANE AUSTEN

In 2020 the world came to a stop during a global pandemic due to a coronavirus called COVID-19. Most businesses and restaurants shut their doors, schools closed, nursing homes and retirement centers stopped allowing visitors, professional sports came to a halt, groceries and paper products became scarce, and most countries issued travel restrictions. People across the world were instructed to stay in their homes and shelter in place, keeping at least a six-foot distance from other people when they did go out. And every day, people voiced their discontent.

However, something else happened that gave rise to a great sense of contentment for the contentment seekers. While the discontented folk complained about everything from being "locked" in their homes to politics to running out of bathroom tissue to being forced to homeschool their children, the contentment seekers shared good news. Air pollution decreased in major cities across the globe. Families reconnected. Life became less harried.

In their personal lives, the contentment seekers . . .

Got caught up on home projects they had been putting off.

Began cooking all of their meals at home and learned new recipes as a result.

Finally had time to start exercising more.

Launched the home-based businesses they always dreamed of.

Began to paint and draw and create and write poetry for the first time.

Threw family dance parties.

Clearly, contentment is a state of mind. It's a choice. The same circumstances can be happening to everyone, and there will always be two camps: the discontent and the content. Which side will you fall on?

97

Practice the Art of Surrender

Don't be afraid to give up the good to go for the great.

—JOHN D. ROCKEFELLER

It is human nature to want to be in control of our own lives—and, if we're honest, sometimes the lives of others. Because we desire control, we must fight to make the choice to surrender moment by moment by moment by moment throughout the day. Such surrendering, like everything else about true contentment, comes more easily with faith in God and intention.

Why surrender? What's the benefit? Surrendering to God and letting go of our perceived control is a way to give up the bad for the good, and the good for the great. It takes faith, for sure, but when we "let go and let God," amazing things start to happen. Generally speaking, our unhealthy patterns are broken. New, healthy habits come alive. It's different and personal for each of us, and it's a topic for you to explore for yourself.

Of course, some things are easier to surrender than others. Answering the following questions will help you identify how readily you choose to surrender:

- As you think about your life, what attitudes, actions, habits, or possessions would you be wise to surrender right now?
- Why are those things relatively easy to surrender?
- What attitudes, actions, habits, or possessions are you reluctant to surrender?

- Why don't you want to give away those things?
- What attitude, action, habit, or possession do you know you absolutely need to let go of?

Letting go of people you love, possessions that comfort you, or dreams you have long pursued is difficult for various reasons. Uncertainty can definitely get in the way.

But the struggle comes down to this: you can debate with yourself and you can argue with God, or you can recognize when it's time to let go. That conclusion—however long it took you to arrive there—may grow and strengthen your faith. You are surrendering something ultimately small in exchange for something much bigger, something you don't yet have, something you probably can't even conceive of.

The reality seems counterintuitive, but the more you surrender, the greater the love, power, and contentment you'll likely experience in life.

98

Take Time to Budget

Beware of little expenses. A small leak will sink a great ship.

—BENJAMIN FRANKLIN

Sitting down to look at your bank balance or bills rarely inspires the idea of contentment. However, just as tidying your home and organizing your office can bring satisfaction and contentment, so can simplifying and neatening up your finances. Working through the following questions will help:

1. What are your recurring expenses? Which of these can you eliminate or cut down on? Think about music subscriptions, cable, online gaming, fitness clubs, and so forth.

2. How often do you eat out? How much do you spend on average each month? Which of your outings can you eliminate? (Your waistline as well as your budget might thank you for making some changes.)

3. How often do you go out for coffee, tea, and/or adult beverages? Financial author David Bach has written about the concept of "the latte factor" in his book of the same name, sharing how these small expenses will sink your bank account. What would happen if you stopped spending in this category for a month?

4. How much do you spend on groceries each week? More important, how much food do you throw away each week? Coming up with a meal plan can help reduce the amount of wasted food and money— and, again, your waistline may thank you.

5. How much credit card debt do you have? According to a 2019 CNBC article, Americans' debt is on the rise. Credit card interest is hitting record highs. I encourage you to pick one credit card and pay it off. That step alone could save you literally hundreds each month in credit card fees.

6. How much do you spend on miscellaneous items and/or online shopping? Consider going on a spending fast. Identify your favorite item to spend money on (mine happens to be books) and put yourself on a temporary spending freeze. Don't buy any items in that particular category. Your fasting may make a difference in your finances and help get you out of a financial hole.

7. Do you have an actual working budget? You'd be surprised to know how many people don't have a budget, and their guesswork creates more discontent than you can imagine. Writing down your budget—and sticking to it—can give you a sense of confidence and contentment.

What financial game can you begin playing this week that will improve your financial situation and therefore be a reason for contentment?

99

Master the Art of Contentment

The great artist is the simplifier.

—VINCENT VAN GOGH

You are an artist in training, and like budding painters do, you can learn by studying the work of such masters as Monet, Picasso, van Gogh, and Dali. Student artists consider each brushstroke, the master's use of perspective and light, and the blending of the colors. The students take what they learn and then infuse it with their own unique style.

You can use a similar process as you master the art of contentment. Take what you've learned from this book and infuse the approach to contentment with your own unique style.

After all, you are a beautiful, unique creation equipped with everything you need to create a contentment style all your own. But remember, like any artist, at times you will be content with what you create, and at times you won't be. So be willing to make changes or to take risks when you feel they are worth taking. And be careful that you don't get too caught up in trying to re-create yourself striving for perfection. Instead, choose to find joy in every step you take toward true contentment. Celebrate the life you have. Be grateful for each blessing God has given you. Learn to walk through life closer to Him.

Jeremiah Burroughs was a seventeenth-century Puritan preacher who had learned the art of true contentment. He wrote this in *The Rare Jewel of Christian Contentment*:

Contentment is to be learned as a great mystery, and those who are thoroughly trained in this art . . . have learned a deep mystery. "I have learned it"—I do not have to learn it now, nor did I have the art at first; I have attained it, though with much ado, and now, by the grace of God, I have become the master of this art.

Burroughs wasn't always truly content, but he studied, he learned, and he mastered it.

You can master the art of contentment too!

LOVE
the
LIFE
you
HAVE

100

Love Your Life

Dare to live the life you have dreamed for yourself.
Go forward and make your dreams come true.

—RALPH WALDO EMERSON

Everyone has days when they feel like giving up. On those days we have an opportunity to take significant steps toward reaching true contentment. You see, on those days, we can choose to look at the outward circumstances or to look upward to God and find contentment—and even joy—in Him.

On those difficult days, ask yourself the following questions:

1. What can I do to feel more content?
2. What can I do to fix those places in my life where I am not at all content?
3. What can I do to live in the moment more often?
4. I have enough, but what can I do to strengthen and maintain that conviction?
5. What specifically can I do to celebrate the good in my life even while I'm working through something difficult?

If you've put into practice some things you've learned in this book, then you're well on your way to mastering the art of true contentment. Remember, life is a work in progress. And learning contentment is an art.

Bibliography

Aesop. A Selection of Stories from the Aesop for Children. Library of Congress. Accessed April 20, 2020. http://www.read.gov/aesop/001.html.

Alexander, James W. "Patience." Project Gutenberg. Release date May 2, 2014. https://www.gutenberg.org/files/45564/45564-h/45564-h.htm.

Bach, David. "The Latte Factor Calculator." DavidBach.com. Site accessed April 20, 2020. https://davidbach.com/latte-factor-backup/.

Baker, Ray Stannard. Adventures in Contentment. Release date January 5, 2004. http://www.gutenberg.org/files/10605/10605-h/10605-h.htm.

Borchard, Therese J. "How Faith Helps Depression." PsychCentral. Last updated July 8, 2018. https://psychcentral.com/blog/how-faith-helps-depression/.

Browning, Robert. "Pippa Passes." Pippa Passes and Shorter Poems. Poem of the Week. Accessed April 20, 2020. http://www.potw.org/archive/potw48.html.

Burroughs, Jeremiah. The Rare Jewel of Christian Contentment. Chapel Library.org. Site accessed April 20, 2020. https://chapellibrary.org:8443/pdf/books/rjoc.pdf.

Chapman, Gary. "The Five Love Languages Defined." The 5 Love Languages. Accessed April 20, 2020. https://www.5lovelanguages.com/2018/06/the-five-love-languages-defined/.

Crane, Frank. "Just for Today." Quote Investigator. Published July 26, 2012. https://quoteinvestigator.com/2012/07/26/just-for-today/.

Dickinson, Emily. "Hope Is a Thing with Feathers." Accessed April 20, 2020. https://poets.org/poem/hope-thing-feathers-254.

Elswit, Sharon Barcan. The Jewish Story Finder: A Guide to 668 Tales Listing Subjects and Sources. McFarland & Company Inc., 2012, p.124.

Emerson, Ralph Waldo. Collected Poems & Translations. GoodReads. Accessed April 20, 2020. https://www.goodreads.com/work/quotes/446551-collected-poems-and-translations-library-of-america.

Fitch, Kimberly and Sangeeta Agrawal. "Female Bosses Are More Engaging than Male Bosses." Forbes. Published May 7, 2015. https://news.gallup.com/businessjournal/183026/female-bosses-engaging-male-bosses.aspx.

Guest, Edgar. "Keep Going." Newspapers.com. Published February 3, 2015. https://www.newspapers.com/clip/1709402/keep-going-poem-by-edgar-a-guest/.

Guest, Edgar A. "Kindness." The Path to Home. Project Gutenberg. Release date June 21, 2007. https://www.gutenberg.org/files/21890/21890-h/21890-h.htm#ph14.

Guild, Caroline. Violet: A Fairy Story. Project Gutenberg. Release date April 5, 2011. http://www.gutenberg.org/files/35773/35773-h/35773-h.htm.

Kiefer, James E. "Gladys Aylward, Missionary to China." Biographical Sketches of Memorable Christians of the Past, sponsored by the Society of Archbishop Justus. Last updated August 29, 1999. http://justus.anglican.org/resources/bio/73.html.

Kilner, Mary Ann. Jemima Placid or, The Advantage of Good Nature. Project Gutenberg. Release date September 23, 2011. http://www.gutenberg.org/files/37514/37514-h/37514-h.htm.

"Lisa Beamer's Strength: Her husband's words became a rallying cry for the nation." NBC News. Updated September 11, 2006. http://www.nbcnews.com/id/3080111/ns/dateline_nbc-newsmakers/t/lisa-beamers-strength/#.Xp4RVC2ZM6g.

Shakespeare, William. The Complete Works of Shakespeare: The Tragedy of Othello, Moor of Venice. Project Gutenberg. Published June 1999. http://www.gutenberg.org/cache/epub/1793/pg1793-images.html.

Stallard, Michael. "Why Women Leaders Are Outperforming Men." Forbes. Published October 19, 2018. https://www.forbes.com/sites/forbescoachescouncil/2018/10/19/why-women-leaders-are-outperforming-men/#4a452fc470eb.

Strang, Alan L. "The Seasons." Public Domain Poetry. Accessed April 20, 2020. http://www.public-domain-poetry.com/alan-l-strang/seasons-36162.

"Time Flies: U.S. Adults Now Spend Nearly Half a Day Interacting with Media." The Nielson Company. July 31, 2018. https://www.nielsen.com/us/en/insights/article/2018/time-flies-us-adults-now-spend-nearly-half-a-day-interacting-with-media/.

"The Wizard of Oz Quotes." Movie Quotes Database. Accessed April 20, 2020. http://www.moviequotedb.com/movies/wizard-of-oz-the/quote_26320.html.

Worstall, Tim. "If You Have $10 and No Debt, You Are Richer than 15% of American Households Put Together." Forbes. Published August 2, 2016. https://www.forbes.com/sites/timworstall/2016/08/02/if-you-have-10-and-no-debt-you-are-richer-than-15-of-american-households-put-together/#6882f52b989e.